Marriage 2.0

How to Create a Relationship in Harmony with Who You Are and the Life You Want

SUSAN MAYGINNES, M.A.

Rising Heart Publishing

Rising Heart Publishing
Copyright © 2011 Susan Mayginnes

ISBN: 0615549721
ISBN-13: 9780615549729

Dedication

For my parents, Nat and Vicki, who have always given me uncondi-
tional love and support throughout my life.

Acknowledgements

I want to thank the teachers who have guided me along my journey and whose teachings have informed my work and are present in the many tools I offer.

In particular I want to thank Gay and Kathlyn Hendricks who opened my eyes to what is really possible in conscious relationships, Ron Bynum and Lloyd Fickett who taught me Generous Listening, Byron Katie for freedom from the story, and the thousands of participants who have been in my workshops over the last 30 years.

I am especially grateful to my friends and family who have supported me through the great times and tough times in my life and relationships: Michael Kramer, Margaret Horton, Diana Sutter, Tina Haller, Amy Cheney, Sam and Cassie Bull. Where would we be without friends?

I also thank my editor Colleen Mauro who was the first person to read my book and encouraged me with her feedback.

Many thanks to the men in my life through whom I learned my many lessons of love and relationships and who have served my growth as a human being.

I am especially grateful for the love and support I have received from all of my step-children through this journey: Shamaz, Mardana, Lana and Dominique. You are the grand prize of all.

Thank you to my friend and business partner, Burke Franklin, with whom I co-created the Marriage 2.0 program and who has been a warrior for the project all the way.

www.Marriage2-0.com

Contents

Introduction

How do you create a relationship that works in the modern world when all of the statistics are stacked against you? How does a couple with full time careers who work long hours create an intimate, thriving and healthy marriage? How do people who are afraid to commit to marriage find the commitment they can make? How do you enter fully into relationship with another person without giving up yourself? How do you let go of trying to constantly secure the future of your relationship and live fully in the present? How do you bring priority to your marriage in the midst of the myriad distractions in modern life? This book will help you answer these questions and guide you into some of the most important conversations that every couple needs to have.

Marriage. People in every country in the world and in all walks of life do it. It is one of the biggest decisions that anyone makes in their lifetime. The search for "the one," is a huge biological and psychological motivator and underlies many of our other choices in life—the career we choose, the clothes we buy, our social activities and how we save or spend our money.

When we finally meet someone who seems to have much of what we want in a mate, we wonder, "Is this the right person for me?" How do we make that decision?

In this book, you will sort out this inquiry in a meaningful way. In over thirty years of counseling couples and leading workshops on relationships, I have found that most of the time people don't know what questions to ask or how to find their way through the landscape of relationship possibilities. Even dating sites that promise to find "ideal matches" for people really only scratch the surface of inquiry. Most of the things that people write in their online profiles have more to do with who they wish they were then who they actually are. As a result, most people's experience of online dating is disappointing, although some people have indeed found "matches." Often we meet people who look good on "paper" but the chemistry we want to feel just isn't there.

It's difficult to look beyond the surface of shared hobbies or sexual preferences to discover the most important factors that determine whether marriage is an appropriate choice.

In this book I will redefine a "successful marriage" as it relates to the "new world." One of the primary difficulties of marriage is that we are still trying to fit it inside of an outdated model that was developed at a time when people lived a very different kind of life. The choices we have today—in career, social activities, creative expression and travel—exceed anything ever seen in history. There are so many options that many of us are afraid that a marriage will mean giving up every other option we have. Many "commitment-phobes" see marriage as a limitation of their freedom rather than an expansion of it and therefore never experience the freedom to commit.

In this book you will learn…

The most important questions you need to ask in order to select a partner that is right for you or questions you need to discuss with the partner you already have.

How to invent the marriage—and the life—that is right for you and your partner.

The three most important skills for making a marriage work.

How to get the most out of your marriage.

In the past thirty years I have had the privilege of conducting hundreds of workshops and retreats for couples and single people interested in relationships. I have worked with thousands of couples on their marriages and their personal challenges, and helped them to create breakthroughs in their experience of themselves, their partners and the relationship. I have seen marriages that were dead come to life and I have seen marriages that were on the brink of ending become solid, loving relationships. I have seen couples who do nothing but fight become couples who can communicate and skillfully navigate their way to a resolution. And I have seen couples who have no business being together finally develop the courage to move on in a way that allows both people to go forward with their lives.

I am not someone who believes that marriage must last forever. I was in an eight year "living together" relationship and after that, a ten-year marriage. I can speak from personal experience to the challenges of marriage—significant differences in lifestyle preferences, earning capacity, age difference, differences in sexual preferences—as well as the impact of the death of a child on a relationship, the loss of a business, the growth of business, financial success, financial loss, step-parenting and divorce.

Marriage is your PhD in life. It is where you will confront the best and the worst of yourself and where you will be asked to really grow and mature as a person. It is where you will experience your greatest joys and deepest sorrows. It will make you vulnerable and open your heart. It will also break your heart at times and trigger your deepest fears.

The Curriculum of Marriage

The purpose of a "marriage curriculum" is be to become clear about who you are, what your values are, what you want, and how to support another person in being fully who they are. You also need to understand how to communicate well, what it means to be a personally responsible adult, and what commitment is and is not. You must learn to open your heart and mind, become emotionally intelligent and let go of trying to control everything. You can explore your sexuality and sexual expression, get good at vulnerability and discover your blind spots. The course I have outlined for you is revolutionary and amazingly practical. It brings marriage into the new world and makes it fail-safe.

During my three decades of research, I read everything I could find on the subject of marriage and practiced these teachings in my own life. I've listened to my clients' relationship complaints and I've seen first hand what works and what doesn't, as well as the appropriateness of selection and the appropriateness of divorce. I have compiled the tools that I—and my clients—have found the most transformational. I've done the research so that you don't have to and I'll teach you the best of what I've found. I will provide you with the power tools for making a relationship work—the thinking, the perspective, the action, practices and skills.

However, having an extraordinary relationship is not the end game. Having an extraordinary life is. Yet, for most of us love and romance are much of what makes our lives rich and meaningful. It adds a dimension to our lives that nothing else does. And yet, you may discover that a relationship that is right for you now may not be right at a different stage of your life. The answer is not to morph yourself into being someone who fits inside of your relationship, but to be the most authentic expression of who you really are and to allow the relationship to grow as you grow. You may find yourself with the same partner for the rest of your life, or you may find that your growth as a person will move you beyond your current relationship. Whether you stay together until "death do you part," is not the point. I think we all go into a marriage with the hope that we will be with our partners forever and ever. That is certainly the story we all grew up with. However, we have no idea if we will. And we have no idea if in a year from now—or ten years from now—we will feel the same way. Marriage doesn't come with a guarantee. And the more we try to "guarantee it" the more constricting and controlling we become of our partners and ourselves.

I want to break the notion of marriage as a pass/fail course or a purchase with a lifetime guarantee. The traditional idea is that if you stay in your marriage, you pass. If you end it, you've failed. Or the product "didn't work." This means that if you stay in a toxic marriage that no longer serves either person you've succeeded; if you have a great relationship experience with someone and then choose to end the marriage for any number of good reasons, you've failed.

I want to break the grip of the existing paradigm and bring marriage up to date with the needs of a modern society and a more enlightened perspective. You may ask, why get married? Why not just live together? And you can. However, as I have seen in my own life, and in the lives of thousands of couples I've worked with, there is a commitment that happens in the context of marriage that is fundamentally different than just living together for most people. Even if it's a marriage outside of the legal system, as in same sex marriages or couples who choose to marry each other in a ceremony outside of "legal" or government channels. It's like the difference between Velcro and glue. It simply has more sticking power in our minds. More gravitas. It also has more "baggage" in that we bring all of our concepts, notions, expectations and assumptions about marriage to the party. This includes all of the unconscious stuff that we have accumulated in our thoughts and belief systems about marriage—what we witnessed growing up, as well as the fantasy relationships we've seen in TV sitcoms and movies.

We never see what happens two years after the hero and heroine fall in love.

We never see their first fight, or how they feel when their relationship patterns are in full swing and they've moved past the idealization that drew them together in the first place. But most of our conscious and unconscious expectations of relationships arise from what we observed of our parents and the way they did marriage. However, this generally lives in our blind spot. Even though we may pick someone who looks different than our mothers or fathers and is different in many ways, we will still find ways to unconsciously duplicate the dynamics of our parent's marriage—as well as elements of our own relationship with our parents—into our marriage.

The opportunity in this is huge. It gives us the opportunity to examine our own thoughts, feelings and behaviors that lead to our experience of marriage. It allows us to see how we unconsciously manipulate people and situations to make things happen in a certain way. When we can use what is happening on the outside to explore what is happening on the inside, it allows us to transform who we are and the quality of our relationships. It also allows us to create the marriage and life we want, not simply the play out of our past. We can invent a new legacy in our lives by innovating a marriage consciously as a collaborative creative partnership.

In each section of the book there are a series of questions with examples. Take the time to think about your own answers and then discuss them with your partner. Some of these will be easy and others may be more challenging. They are designed to open up conversations that allow us to see deeper into each other and even challenge our own thinking. Remember, everything that you currently think about marriage is something that you learned–in other words, someone else's idea. This is the opportunity to challenge the existing set of assumptions and generate your own ideas for your relationship.

1
Marriage:
What It Is and Why We Need It

I grew up in the fifties in a neighborhood in the Bronx. My parents, older brother and I lived in a two- bedroom apartment on The Grand Concourse. My aunt Miriam lived upstairs and my grandmother and uncle Steve lived across the street. My cousin Claire and Sharon and Lisa, her two daughters who were my age, lived close by. My cousin Sidney, his wife Francis and their four daughters who were like sisters to me, were also close by. I also had a variety of other aunts, uncles and cousins a short drive or bus ride away. If someone wasn't happy with me on any given day, I could always go over to someone else's house and feel loved and accepted. In addition, there were many other families with kids my age in our apartment building. We shopped in small specialty stores with vendors who knew me and my family—the man who worked at the produce store, the lady who owned the bakery who always had a cookie for me, the guys at the meat market and the small local grocer. This was my community. Just two generations ago, this type of community was a fact of life.

Today my friends, kids and family members are scattered all over the United States and even live in foreign countries due to career opportunities, travel options and other journeys of life. We stay in touch as best we can through the various technologies available— phone calls, Skype, e-mails, text messaging and every once in a while, an in-person visit. Community, as I knew it growing up, no longer exists.

When I was a kid, the only divorce in our entire family was my cousin Claire. Back then, it was a big deal because it was so unusual. Everyone else who had ever been married and was now single was widowed. Marriage was supposed to be "till death do you part." When we moved to the suburbs all of our neighbors were tradi- tional families—two parents, two or more children and a variety of pets. We had lots of playtime and activities with the other families and their kids. The neighbors helped each other in many ways, including looking after each others' kids. Marriage and family appeared solid. Marriage and family was unquestioned. Marriage and family was a fact of life. Of course this spoke nothing of the quality of marriage, the general state of happiness or well-being of both partners, or the myriad affairs that were going on behind the scenes. People stayed together…no matter what. If there were problems, they worked them through, waited for things to get bet- ter, or just learned to live with them.

Today 60% of marriages end in divorce. The rate of separations among couples who live together is even higher. That doesn't take into account the couples who are separated but still married, or the ones who stay together in totally dysfunctional relationships. It also doesn't take into consideration the general state of HAPPINESS of couples. Most children now live in single parent homes, while other couples struggle over how to stay together as they try to fit them- selves into a model of marriage that is outdated and inappropriate for today. Many people feel dissatisfied in their marriages and feel guilty for feeling dissatisfied. We feel like something is wrong with us—or our partner—if we are unhappy. What we need to do is to shift the question from "What's wrong with me?" or "What's wrong with my partner?" To questioning the way we "do" marriage.

Since a marriage is a union of two separate individuals who live and breathe and change, so too is a marriage a living, breathing, changing organism. And it should be one that represents the evolution of both partners. People have changed since the institution of marriage was first originated. Who we are as a culture, what we want and expect, the demands on us, our dreams and aspirations, our challenges in life and the circumstances in which we live are different than it was a hundred years ago or even fifty years ago. Not only have people, towns, neighborhoods and families changed, but the entire culture has shifted as well.

New Forms for New Realities

These changes are not all bad. Although neighborhoods were much smaller and tighter in the past, so were opportunities for growth— personally, professionally and economically. People may have stayed together, but there were many unhappy marriages and many individuals whose personal and professional growth were deeply compromised by remaining in a marriage that operated within a narrow set of parameters about what a marriage was or wasn't supposed to be. They were also compromised by a general lack of open communication and discussion around everything from careers, money, sex, life style, children, feelings, emotions and deep thought.

Couples and families were expected to operate within the general rules of what was expected in their communities and risked being ostracized for behaviors and choices that deviated from the norm, such as interracial marriage, religious choices, or other outside the norm options such as stay-at-home dads, or divorce. "If a marriage was unhappy," writes John Welwood in Journey of the Heart, "community pressure would hold it together... Now, for the first time in history, every couple is on their own to discover how to build a healthy relationship, and to forge their own vision of how and why to be together."

We are pioneers of a new era in which every couple can create a version of marriage that works best for them. The high divorce rate is evidence that traditional models of marriage are no longer working, although there are elements of the tradition that we may wish to maintain. But the old model of marriage with all of its assumptions, is inadequate for dealing with all of the new possibilities for love, intimacy, communication, personal growth and prosperity that exist in our world today. Fewer marital partners are willing to be a "half" of a whole (even if it's "the better half!") or to let gender dictate their roles and responsibilities.

One of the things that people want in relationship today is the opportunity to explore different possible roles and responsibilities that work best for them, rather then just acting out traditional roles. In a highly fragmented world with a fragmented sense of community, a healthy, high functioning marriage provides a powerful base of support. It offers a place of belonging, a conscious loving sense of family, and a stable ground from which to grow and to live out our personal missions in life. It is a strong supportive base—much like the communities of yesteryear—where we have someone we can count on who counts on us, someone who knows and loves us, a partner with whom we can journey through life. The world can be a difficult and challenging place, and it is good to have a home where we can rest and feel nurtured and supported. In this book, we will embark on a journey of designing a marriage that is a fit for who you are, who your partner is, and the personal and professional lives you wish to lead.

We will look at all of the components that create a close intimate partnership and all of the options available to you. We will put up for examination all of the "sacred cows" of traditional marriage and your own ideas and assumptions. We will explore possibilities and choices that are a reflection of the person you are today and the person you wish to become. Over time you will be able to use this book to review those choices and update them for your evolving partnership. As you and your life change, it is appropriate to re-look at the "terms and conditions" of your marriage contract and to update them as you both grow and evolve. Therefore, I recommend that your marriage contract include an "annual review" which will allow you to look at your choices and agreements and make the appropriate changes as you re-commit to the marriage. I know one couple who do this each year and they have been in a happy, high-functioning marriage for over twenty years!

My Story

I was married for ten years. We were introduced by a mutual friend at a personal growth seminar on the subject of relationships. We fell in love almost instantly and I moved in with him two weeks later. I had been involved with personal growth work both personally and professionally for years and was thrilled to meet a man who was also interested in personal growth. He had four children and I was delighted to be a step-mom, as I had not had children at this point in my life. Over the next few years we enjoyed an almost blissful existence. We had challenges in life, but we worked as a team to overcome adversity and every challenge brought us closer together. We lived on his property in Mendocino in an idyllic setting of forest and mountains, and even though he was in the midst of a turbulent divorce, our time together was almost storybook. Things actually went along this way for about eight years. There was very little we argued about, as we were like-minded on so many issues. Aside from the challenges and difficulties that we faced in life such as the loss of a business and the loss of my stepson who died in a car accident, our relationship was the solid ground on which we both stood. We were both very affectionate and loved to do things for each other.

Living in an isolated environment (107 acres in a wilderness area) made us even closer. Other than children, pets and the wildlife that migrated through our property, we had few others around on a regular basis. We had each other and life was great.

Flash forward eight years …

> *"We must let go of the life we have planned,*
> *so as to accept the one that is waiting for us."*
> - Joseph Campbell

In the middle of my life my life took an interesting turn. I had just stepped off the plane from a trip to Europe that I had taken with my mother and brother and was totally exhausted from travel and lack of sleep. My husband picked me up at the airport and drove me home. I was beyond happy to see him, I had missed him terribly. The loving emails and phone calls I received from him while I was gone confirmed our love and desire to be together. When we got home, he drew a bath for me. I sank into the warm water and relaxed.

"I have something to tell you," he said, sitting down.

I looked at him curiously.

"I had sex with Mimi."

What little wind I had left in me after twenty-four hours of travel and jet lag sucked out of my lungs. I felt numbness creeping into a hollow place that formed in the pit of my stomach. I sank down into the water. Everything in me sank down. My life as I knew it sank down.

A rush of feelings, images, thoughts. Then blank. My mind stopped. I saw the steam rising from the bath water, the light reflecting the gold fixtures. I saw his face. It was tense and looking at me. He seemed calm and collected, except for his face.

Mimi was a long-time friend of my husband. In fact, they had had an affair during his first marriage. (Yes, I'd married someone with a track record of marital affairs!) They had "run into each other" more recently at an event, had "stayed in touch" and even visited one another. I had asked him if there was anything going on and he said, "absolutely not." Although I intuitively sensed that something was happening, his strong denial allowed me to override my own instincts. I preferred to believe what I was hearing rather then what I instinctively knew.

I had told myself long ago that if this ever happened I would leave. Now here it was. What was I going to actually do? What does one say in this situation? All that would come out was "When?"

I wanted details—what, when, where, why. I don't know why I wanted the details—it's the last thing most people want. I think I wanted to prove that it wasn't true.

Finding out that my husband had had an affair with his old friend was like finding out that I had been living in Beirut, after believing that I'd been in California for ten years. It seemed impossible. The way I thought the world was had nothing whatsoever to do with the way it actually was. Everything felt surreal. I was in shock.

Sleep deprivation from travel turned into three more days of sleeplessness. I could not eat or sleep. All I could do was cry or feel numb. My mind was filled with images of "them." I was distraught and in more emotional pain that I had ever known. In addition, I been a teacher for many years on the subject of relationships and I thought, "Great, I can just see the headlines now: Husband Cheats on Relationship Teacher."

> *"In the middle of the road of my life I awoke in the dark wood*
> *where the true way was wholly lost"*
> *- Dante Alighieri from Le Comedia* Ending & Beginnings

Months of couples therapy and conversation ensued. Eventually, I was able to forgive my husband. I found insight into myself, and into him and we worked on shifting the dynamics of our relationship that were subtly problematic. I let go of the affair and was happy to get on with my marriage. Or so I thought.

It was two years before the next affair. When he told me this time, I knew it was over. But when his pattern was identified as "love and sex addiction," I felt I needed to be supportive as he went through therapy and a twelve-step program. Like many women, I had "hope" that the situation could be resolved. I hoped that that his problem was fixable. I hoped that there was some way that "if we did all the right things" our marriage would work out. Eventually, I had to face the fact that to stay in the marriage was a commitment to drama and to keeping an old belief about myself alive. I packed up and moved out. I wasn't angry, I just knew that I could not help him with the next part of his journey and that it was unhealthy for me to stay. The situation had become toxic to my well-being and the marriage was over.

Although this was a gruelingly difficult choice it was the best thing I did. Six years later, my ex-husband and I are good friends. His new girlfriend is also a friend and I love their new baby. Six years ago I couldn't imagine that I'd ever feel this way. Now, it's hard to imagine feeling any differently. I will share my journey of how I got there with you.

> *"The biggest factor in being happy is a person's ability to shift his state of mind."*
> - John Hopkins Research

Revelation

In the end, what I realized is this: Life has a way of showing us what we need to see. I had to face the fact that I had compromised on what I'd wanted for years. I'd felt "stuck" in the marriage because I did love him and was afraid of leaving. I believed that if you loved someone, there could be no other reason to leave. I had given up so many elements of what mattered to me in life—my lifestyle, my work, my contribution to a larger world, my independence, my social life, my friends and extended family—in order to fit into his world and try to make it mine. Our remote location kept me isolated from friends and family members. I found it almost impossible to continue to do my consulting work in any significant way and I struggled with this the entire time.

Although there were many beautiful aspects of that lifestyle, I thrive on relationships, community and interaction and collaboration with others. There is a great line in the movie, **Out of Africa**, where Meryl Streep says something to Robert Redford like, "I don't want to get to the end of my life and realize I've lived somebody else's dream." If none of this had happened, I might have done exactly that. I was simply scared to face the reality of the compromise I had made because of what I might lose—which in the end, I lost anyway. And in the process, I gained back my Self and my life.

2

The Theatre of Life or "What the Hell is This Play Doing on My Stage?"

As my life unfolds, I often feel like I'm entering a theatre in the middle of a three-act play. I have an idea of where I've been and only a thought about where I am going. I know there is a storyline with a beginning and an end. But all I really know is that I am in the middle of the scene that is playing right now. My life has never gone according to plan. The life I am living is radically different—and fundamentally better—then anything I could have imagined. I've realized that my life has always given me exactly what I needed—even when I didn't know I needed it. It has pointed me in a specific direction, or it has pointed me inward for a deeper truth, for something more real then the mental movie. When things don't go according to plan our first response is to get upset. My marriage was one example of that for me. The emotional difficulty of it invited—no, demanded—that I go deep into myself, to see what was arising from my own depths and to explore with great interest "What the hell is this play doing on my stage?!"

In my work with couples, I invite people to look at why a particular storyline may be appearing in the novel of their life. In other words, what is it about their past and their perception of themselves and relationships that would make a particular storyline likely to occur?

In my own exploration I saw that I had deep seeded ideas that no man would really want to commit to just me. My father was someone who really enjoyed the gifts and talents of children and I often heard him say great things about other kids. I just never heard him say great things about me. I remembered looking in a mirror at the age of six or so and wondering why my dad found the little girl next door so cute, and not me. She was short, blond and blue-eyed. I was tall, skinny and gangly. I figured out that whatever she was was cute, and whatever I was, wasn't. As children, our perceptions are limited; what we see it is not necessarily the whole story. What we "figure out" as children may lack perspective. In fact, years later, my uncle told me that I was "the apple of my father's eye." I was surprised; I hadn't figured that out. But the impact of my perception, whether true or not, created a subconscious belief that men would always find other women more appealing than me. And as a result, that has been my experience.

To become aware of our unconscious beliefs and to go within and to begin to explore and challenge them creates personal transformation. It is the opportunity to "harvest the gold" from anything that shows up in our lives. For me, it was a personal epiphany in which the assumptions of my life became transparent. As I began to see through my fundamental misconceptions about men, relationships and my own "lovability," new possibilities arose. This allowed me to step into a new level of personal responsibility, and to make choices that were more in alignment with the kind of life and relationships I wanted to create. I stopped selecting the people who only reinforced the old idea and began to bring people and situations into my life that supported a new experience. I began to show up in my relationships as someone with a different possibility. It allowed me to drop my "story" about life and come directly into it. I realized that my divorce had blown my "you and me off into the sunset forever" storyline. This was the story I'd grown up with and this was the way "it was supposed to be." I was supposed to make that storyline work—reality be damned.

I think one of the most dangerous things we can do is to try to make something unworkable work out. We can hope for something better and make something "workable" that is basically wrong for us. We do this with relationships, jobs, friends and other situations. We can stay forever in the wrong situation because we don't want to admit that it is the wrong situation.

Which takes me to the work of this book. How do you make it more likely that you will create a situation or relationship that is "right" for you and the life you want? What do you need to know? As I've mentioned, I have used the skills in this book with hundreds of couples and have seen them create extraordinary results in each and every relationship. I've also seen people like myself who decide to not continue their marriages develop the skills to create a positive, loving relationship with their ex's based on new agreements and new understanding.

Know Thyself

How do we fully participate in marriage without giving up ourselves? The key is to "know thyself" and to craft and continue to re-craft a marriage that is less of a compromise and more of a co-creative joint venture. It means becoming very honest with yourself and your partner about what you really want, what works for you and what doesn't. It means facing the truth about yourself and facing—and resolving—any problems before they become insurmountable.

This book will help you to do this. As you read through the book, you will find fun, interesting and engaging discussions and exercises. They will make you think more deeply, and introduce you to new concepts and ideas.

As I've mentioned, I have worked with hundreds of couples who have experienced transformation in marriages that were troubled, stale, at an impasse, or over. In fact, any marriage worth its weight will hit a wall. The wall is the opportunity to face into something new. It's actually not a wall—it's a mirror. The mirror tells us that our current state of operations may need an overhaul. The wall/mirror brings us face to face with not only our partners, but more importantly, with ourselves. It takes us to the place inside where our work can begin. When this happens, the mirror becomes a door we can walk through. One of the greatest opportunities of relationships is the possibility for growth. Growth can consist of many things: our own self-knowledge, our ability to communicate, our understanding of the dynamics of our relationship, our ability to be more intimate, our ability to shift states of mind or points of view, our intuitive skills, our ability to be affectionate and more open sexually, our ability to feel more deeply and express our feelings in healthy ways, our capacity for deep play and real fun, the exploration of our power, our ability to take control and our ability to let go.

I have seen many marriages, including my own, that were an important journey with a fellow traveler for a period of time. And there came a time when it was appropriate for both people to move on for their own growth and happiness. And I have also seen people repeat the same problematic patterns over and over again with new people, because they had never learned what they needed to learn about themselves, or change anything about the way that they "do" relationship.

When we come to the end of our lives, what we remember are relationships and the people who have meant the most to us— not the time we spent at work or recreational activities, or how much money we've made, or the number of hours we've billed. It's the people in our lives that matter most. Since we are here to be in relationship with others, and since this seems to be the most important element our lives, and what truly makes life rich, we may as well get good at it. It's time to commit yourself to being the kind of person who can have the kind of relationship that you want to have.

Welcome to Marriage2-0.

3
Knowing Your Partner's Love Language

"He loves me, he loves me not."

Marriages can be successful if only people would _____.

When you fill in the blank with your own answer, you begin to reveal your own personal formula for what makes you feel loved. Couples who understand the secret love language of their partners have the ability to effectively make each other feel loved and cherished throughout their relationship. They know the little things and big things that are meaningful to their partners. Quite often our partners speak a different love language. It frustrates us when they don't understand that we are expressing love to them in our own way. To them, it is a foreign language. If you want to form a relationship with someone from another country, learning their language would be a crucial factor. The same is true in the "language of love." We each speak a different love language and it is important to learn your partner's language and to have them understand yours. If we want them to feel our love we must express it in their own language.

In the book, **The 5 Love Languages**, Gary Chapman, a psychologist with a background in anthropology describes the five primary "love languages."

1. <u>Words of Affirmation</u>: Verbal compliments, saying the words "I love you."

2. <u>Quality Time</u>: Being fully present, giving your partner your undivided attention, creating mutually enjoyable activities.

3. <u>Receiving Gifts</u>: The giving of special gifts that let your partner know you were thinking of them.

4. <u>Acts of Service</u>: Doing things that help your partner such as taking care of the car, making a meal, vacuuming, paying the bills, trimming the lawn, dealing with insurance company, etc.

5. <u>Physical Touch</u>: Holding hands, kissing, hugging, foreplay, sex, a shoulder rub, a touch of the hand or foot.

Of course most of us enjoy all of these things! However, look and see if there is one in particular that makes you feel the most loved. It is easy to project our own love language onto our partners. For example, if words of affirmation make us feel loved, we may compliment our partner verbally, which they may enjoy. However, if their primary love language is physical touch, they won't ultimately feel loved by our compliments unless they are accompanied with a good dose of touch! On the other hand, if you are very affectionate with your partner and spend time with them, you may think you are showing your love. Consider this familiar conversation:

She: "You don't love me!"

He: "How can you say that?"

She: "You never say it."

He: "Yeah, but I'm HERE aren't I?"

In that example, she likes to be told, and he believes his being there is all that is needed as "proof" of love.

What we complain about not getting from our partners may be an important indicator of how we each get our "love messages." For example, if my partner is always complaining that I'm "never there," "I work too much," "I'm not present," etc., that may be a good indicator that they value quality time as a way of feeling loved. If my partner complains that "I don't do enough around the house" or that "I didn't take care of something" that mattered to them, that may indicate that acts of service are a key indicator of love to them.

When I was in Spain last year, a man came up to me on the street and said something in Spanish. My Spanish is pretty basic, so I turned to my friend Amy and said, "I think he's TRYING to say..." and told her what I thought. She looked at me, smiled and corrected my perspective: "No, he's not TRYING to say that, he IS saying that. You are TRYING to understand!" We both laughed at the tendency to think ego-centrically.

Answer these questions to begin to identify your own love language:

In what way do you most often express love to others?
Doing things for them
Offering praise and acknowledgement
Getting them something special
Spending extra time with them, giving them attention
Being physically affectionate

In what way does your partner most often express love to you? In what of the above categories does that seem to fit?

Notice the difference between you and your partner in this area. Often, these preferences come from what we got from our parents growing up, or conversely, what we didn't get from our parents. For example, if your father never told you that he loved you but instead showed you by doing things for you or joking around with you, those might be ways in which you know that you are loved.

On the other hand, what you may most want is someone who can tell you verbally. Also notice how our parenting shapes the way in which we show love. Because we grew up in different homes, the way in which we understand or receive love may be very different for each of us. How often do you hear the classic story of someone complaining that their husband or wife doesn't love them while the spouse sits there looking completely frustrated or perplexed because they don't understand why their partners feel so unloved? Speaking your partner's "language" in love is key. Learn how your partner really "hears" the language of love and put time and attention into doing that. It will create a loving environment in your home.

To explore this further, pick up a copy of The Five Love Languages by Dr. Gary Chapman. It's a relationships book classic that will give you a lot of insight into this area and help you translate your partner's "language." Again, we think that the way we like to *express* love is how our partner *receives* love. You will discover in your conversation with them that this is often not the case. They may enjoy your expression of love but there is often something else that someone needs to really experience being loved. It is important not to take this personally or have this mean something problematic about you or them. Anymore then it would mean something if you went to a foreign country and they did not fully understand your language. This is a surprising realization for most couples but the discussion of this really allows us to find out how we can create an environment of love for our partner and what we really want from them.

Question your assumptions!

4
Knowing Your Partner's Likes & Dislikes

A big part of knowing someone over time is learning about what they like and what they dislike, what they love and what they hate.

Let's see how much you know about your partner and what things would be important for you to find out!

Answer these questions:

My partner's favorite things to do are:
My partner's favorite things to do with me are:
My favorite things to do are:
My favorite things to do with him/her are:

Notice if you have different "favorite things" with each other, which may also be different than the things you like to do with other people or by yourselves. More than likely you do. Can you answer correctly for your partner? Do you think they know what you like? Sometimes things are obvious to us but may not be to them. Couples often assume they know certain things about each other and are later surprised to find out that their assumptions are wrong. One husband that I worked with told me that his wife loved it when he would order her meal for her at a restaurant. In fact, she resented it but had put up with it for years rather than argue! In another couple, the wife made oatmeal for her husband every day thinking he really liked oatmeal. In fact, he did not like oatmeal particularly but didn't want to say anything about it since she'd been making it for him for fifteen years! She had started making oatmeal for him when they first got married and he never wanted to complain about it.

Let's see how much you know about your partner. Answer these questions (note: throughout this book whenever the choice is "other", make sure you write down your ideas of what that would be):

If I wanted to give my partner a gift they would really appreciate it would be:

Examples:

> *Something practical*
> *A gadget*
> *Clothing or lingerie*
> *Jewelry*
> *Other*

If they wanted to give me something I'd want it to be:

Examples:

> *Something practical*
> *A gadget*
> *Clothing or lingerie*
> *Jewelry*
> *Other*

If I wanted to take my partner somewhere special it would probably be:

Examples:

A spa
A fine restaurant
Out for a wild night of dancing
On a hike
Other

If he/she wanted to take me somewhere special I'd want it to be:

Examples:

To a spa
To a fine restaurant
Out for a wild night of dancing
On a hike
Other

Again notice any differences here. We often buy something for someone that we want. This happens often around birthdays and Christmas which is why department stores invented gift receipts— so people can return the gifts they receive. One of my clients received a beautiful necklace from her husband. It was a very nice necklace, but not at all the kind of jewelry she wears! It was very bright and sparkly and she prefers more conservative pieces. She was shocked that he would pick that out for her and it exemplified to her how little he knew about her tastes and preferences. She was actually offended by the necklace even though she understood that he meant well. When she went back to the store to exchange it, she found nothing that matched her taste and ended up giving the necklace away as a gift. If you are in doubt, but want to get your partner a piece of jewelry, ask one of their close friends to help pick it out. You can also surprise them by taking them to a jewelry store and asking them to pick something out for themselves.

Taking It Deeper

To take the conversation deeper, begin to wonder and discuss *why* these are things you like and don't like. Sometimes we just don't know! But often times we have meanings and significance to these things. For example, I like it when my partner picks up the check at dinner because it makes me feel special and taken care of. Even though I pay half the bills at home or buy the groceries, I like being taken out to dinner rather than taking them out or "splitting it." Sometimes these are things that really bring us to question our assumptions and ideas or habitual ways of thinking, and other times it may just be something that is really important to us. See what the significance is to things you and your partner like. It helps us to understand them more and to understand their preferences and why that is important to them so we can support each other.

To take the conversation further, what are some things that you may have never tried but think you might enjoy? What are some things that you think you would not like but have never actually tried? For example, I never thought I would like skiing. When I was married, my husband was an avid skier so being a "good sport" off to the bunny slope I went! To my surprise, I loved skiing! In fact I stayed out on the slopes until I was able to come down a more advanced run and couldn't wait to get back out the next day. When I looked at why I thought I would not enjoy skiing, it was really because I thought I would be clumsy, I would look bad in the eyes of my husband and kids and I assumed I would not be good at it. Plus I hate being cold! When I could discuss that and realized they didn't really care how I looked as long as I was willing to give it a try, I was game. And I never felt cold!

So look at the things you don't like or the things you think you would not enjoy. Why don't you like those things and why do you think you would not enjoy something? Again, this is just to explore our thinking and the meanings that we put to things, which is often the source of why we like or don't like things.

Question your assumptions!

Likes & dislikes worksheet

Fill in the blank with as many things as you can think of. Write fast and don't edit:

I love it when my partner:

_____

_____

_____

I hate it when my partner:

_____

_____

_____

If I were to tell the truth, what I really want from them is:

_____

_____

_____

If they wanted to know what they could do for me that would be special for my birthday it would be:

_____

_____

_____

My idea of a perfect date with my partner would be:

_____

_____

_____

Answer these questions:

My Pet Peeves are...

Examples:

> *When they leave their shoes lying around the house and I trip over them*
> *Underwear hanging on the doorknob*
> *When they are late and don't call*
> *When they squeeze the toothpaste tube in the middle*

These are a few of my favorite things:

Examples:

> *When they hold my hand as we walk down the street*
> *When he/she stops what they are doing and looks at me when I'm talking to them*
> *A shoulder rub in the evening...*

Ask your partner what their answers are to these questions. You can bring it up while out on a walk together, over a cup of coffee or even lying in bed. Find out what they love, what really bugs them, and what they want.

5
Quality Time

One of the things that people talk about in relationships today is spending "quality time" together. Quality time has become a desired commodity since couples today lead pretty busy lives. Often they each have full time careers and children to devote time to, as well as a host of friends, family and other personal obligations. Spending quality time together keeps us from becoming "passing ships," or from getting so distracted by our lives that we soon find we are married to distraction rather than to each other! One woman complains that her husband comes home from work and is too tired to help with the kids or to have a conversation. He plops down in front of the TV and falls asleep. Another man complains that his girlfriend, an attorney who works six to seven days a week, does not come home until late at night and is too tired to make love.

It is therefore important to discuss what "quality time" means to each of you. And to then schedule it into your lives, rather then to wait for a big chunk of time to magically appear when everything else on your list is done and you now have "time for the relationship." Remember, we do many things in our lives so that we can have a relationship! We earn a living, take care of our appearance (exercise, get your haircut, etc), buy nice outfits, develop ourselves as a person, etc. Don't forget to actually have the relationship! Think of all the things you have done in life just to become the kind of person who can have one. Be sure to not miss it. Schedule time to be with your partner in ways that are meaningful and enjoyable for both of you.

Answer these questions:

To me, quality time means...

Examples:

> *Watching TV or a movie together*
> *An activity where we pay attention to each other*
> *Playing a game together*
> *Having meaningful conversations*
> *Other*

To my partner quality time would be...

Examples:

> *Watching TV or reading the paper together*
> *An activity where we pay attention to each other*
> *Playing a game together*
> *Having meaningful conversations*
> *Other*

Now compare your answers with your partner's answers. What can you do to support or make space for each other's preferences? What are some of the things you can stop doing that aren't really on board with what either of you really enjoy. One of my clients loves to watch television. But it interferes with the amount of intimate time with her husband. So she agreed to watch no more then an hour of television a night and not to watch it at all one night a week. Instead they use that time to do things they BOTH enjoy.

Taking It Deeper

But now let's go a step farther and challenge the conventional thinking about how couples are *supposed* to spend their time together.

Our cultural upbringing dictates that we grow up and get a job/career, get married, move in together, have sex 3 times a week, have 2.5 children, 1.5 pets, and retire by a certain age and die by a certain age. That's the conventional societal script.

I would like to invite you to challenge convention. This "rulebook" for life and relationships is not actually written anywhere but it is "written" into our minds through everything we've grown up with in our society. However, you really can make up the rules the way you want them and the way that works for *your* relationship and *your* life. For example, I know one couple who have been together for 25 years, maintained separate residences, never even bothered to get married and were together until her death at the age of 90 years old! I remember when I found out that they weren't married and had separate households. I was surprised because people of that generation generally had more traditional relationships. Another couple I know who have been married for over 30 years have always maintained 2 separate houses although they are usually over at one together most evenings. Yet at other times they opt to be in their own homes. People require varying amounts of individual time as well as closeness. It's important to find ways to honor these needs in yourself and in each other.

The point is that you can really create this any way you want. Living together is an option regardless of whether or not you are married. Getting legally married is of course an option. Two of my closest friends have been happily married without a license for 15 years. They've both been married before and have some extenuating financial challenges that make legal marriage a bad option for them but have had a "wedding" or sacred ceremony, with exchange of vows in the witness of friends.

Some people have very busy careers that are at the forefront of their lives. When you start getting into the question of creating balance, it raises an interesting question. It does not mean that we put equal amounts of time into the various categories of our lives. Sometimes balance means that you are spending an enormous amount of time getting work done, little time on your social life and small amounts of time with your significant partner. Then your situation can alter and all of a sudden you have a redistribution of your time. You are now able to make large amounts of time available for yourself and your partner and work takes a back seat. In other words, the question is not what has you balanced "out there", but what has you feel balanced *inside of yourself.* By balanced I mean **unconflicted.** When I am at work, I am not at work wishing I was home. When I am home I am not at home wishing I was at work getting more done. I am where I am. The amount of time that I am there is totally up to me. And that may change quite a bit as life changes, situations change and demands change. There is no "correct" amount of time that you spend at work vs. spend at home. There is no significance to the amount of time you spend in one place more than the other. It doesn't have to *mean something*, good or bad. The *problem* is that we usually want to invent problematic meanings about it: This means you don't really love me. This means you don't really care about your job. This means that you're irresponsible. This means that you are being responsible. Where we feel really motivated and drawn to place our attention is fine as long as it works for you and as long as you can have a partner that that also works for. The point is to be fully present wherever you are. For example if you have a spouse that works very long hours and has a job that required an enormous amount of attention, then there will be time where he/she will opt by choice or by necessity to spend a lot of time working and have little time for the relationship other than chunks here and there. In order for this to work, you need a pretty independent partner who has plenty to do and plenty of friends and support without you and doesn't require a lot of attention. Maybe someone who is equally work-focused. If you are someone who requires a fair amount of attention from your partner and really gets your energy and sense of balance from a lot of partner time, that kind of a situation won't work for you. You will feel neglected, left out, abandoned, or alone. You will begin to feel resentful and put significance to the situation such as "this means he doesn't really love me." Or "I guess I'm just not that important to her." You will invent meanings that justify your resentment and then blame your partner. You will become strategic in your attempt to manipulate them to spend more time with you. You may become threatening or whiney. You may even be cold or negative when they are actually with you which of course makes them have even less desire in spending more time with you.

So you have to be honest with yourself and your level of need for attention and time together. If you want a lot of "together time" with your partner, that's great. Just make sure that you find a partner that is available for that physically and emotionally.

Again, there are no right answers. It is whatever the two of you can invent that works for both of you. But you have to question your assumptions about the amount of time you *expect* to be together, doing what, and why. And then formulate agreements that make sense and really work for you *and allow you to be fully present wherever you are.* Create time agreements that you can keep, as breaking agreements is generally a big set up for drama and resentment. Be open to communicate as situations change and you want to renegotiate your time together or your living situation. Eventually we must realize that we create our lives – our careers, our relationships and our activities in life are constructed by us. To have balance is to create situations that can work in harmony with each other as we juggle our responsibilities, our desires and the needs of others in our lives. This takes awareness, communication and flexibility. People with rigid, fixed positions in relationships generally find themselves in power struggles and have difficulty working in collaborative ways – a key to successful relationships.

So ask yourself: What would be ideal? How would I organize my time if I was only considering what I really wanted to do? What really makes me happy? What energizes me? What creates a sense of peace and being present in my life?

Then discuss this with your partner and see how they would answer the questions. What will work lives in the discussion of what can work for *both* of you.

Another thing to notice in these conversations and throughout your conversations in this book is: Am I only thinking within the current conditions? In other words, a lot of times when we try to negotiate solutions, we think within the current set of conditions that we are in, rather than in how we would like it to be. So if I have a job where I work 60 to 80 hours a week, is that something that I enjoy and want to do or am I assuming that I am stuck with that? In Tim Ferriss's best selling book, The Four Hour Work-week, he describes numerous scenarios and examples of people who changed their entire lives to be able to work significantly less and actually improve their lifestyle. He challenges conventional thinking about jobs, money and the cultural assumptions of how we work and why. In the new economy that we are in, thinking outside the box and creatively is crucial. People who will thrive in life are people who can challenge conventional thinking, learn new ideas and invent their own futures.

Open Pandora's Box in your discussion of how you each spend your time at work, socially and at home with each other. One of my clients realized that she always took on lots of volunteer work in order to "be a good person" but that it was robbing her of her time with her partner and doing things for herself like exercising and eating properly. She cut back her volunteer work to one charity that she felt strongly about and handed off her other positions in various organizations. It is important not to be judgmental of each other's use of time but to really look at **what makes you happy**? What energizes you? What "adds life" to you rather than sucks the life out of you? What requests do you have of each other for time together?

This is a rich conversation to have with your partner. It brings up for question many of our assumptions about work, play, relationships and lifestyle. Don't try to come to any immediate conclusions, just "fluff up" the conversation. This is a big exploration. For the next month, at the end of each day ask yourself and your partner these questions:

1. What made me happy today?
2. Where did I experience peace and comfort today?
3. Who or what inspired me today?

These questions come from The Blessing Way taught by Angeles Arrien, author of The Four-Fold Way. They invite you to really see what consistently is your source of happiness, peace and inspiration. This will help you both construct your lives so that you have more joy and inspiration in it and less stress and inner conflict. It will allow you to shape your time so that it works for both of you.

Challenge your assumptions!

6
Appreciation & Acknowledgement

In at least half of the relationships that I have facilitated, people complain about not feeling appreciated by their partner in some way. Think about the word appreciate for a moment. It means "to increase in value." When we have an investment that appreciates, it's value increases. It's important to create an ongoing flow of appreciation in your relationship. As you appreciate your partner, their value to you increases! It is an answer to the question, "Is the cup half full or half empty?" If the cup is half full, you can enjoy what's in the cup. If the cup is half empty, all you feel is scarcity and resentment about what you don't have. Appreciation is a result of where you choose to place your attention. For example, most of us have a tendency to place our attention on problems—the things that are "wrong," what we don't like. As a result, we tend to not notice or take for granted the things that we do appreciate and enjoy. This leaves us with a distorted view of our situation and the feeling that something is always wrong or missing. It is a choice to live in a state of perpetual dissatisfaction. If you have ever had the experience of someone focusing on all of the things they don't like about you, you know the experience of feeling depreciated! It is very dissatisfying for both of you! It's like when you take a new car off the lot and it immediately depreciates in value. Not because the car is any different, but because it's no longer considered "new." As soon as we get someone home, we begin to find all of the things about them that bug us! "Gee, I never noticed that they chew so loudly before..." or, "Wow, they always leave the cap off the toothpaste tube!" or, "I hate it when they leave the seat up in the bathroom..."

When we focus on all of the little things that bother us, our relationship becomes an ongoing experience of annoyance or disappointment. Remember that the mind is threatened by love and intimacy. It is scary to us—consciously or unconsciously—because of the feelings of vulnerability that it exposes. The "mind" is that sometimes loud and sometimes soft voice that you hear playing in your head all the time, like a radio playing in the background of your life. It's tricky, because the voice is very similar to your own so you think it's really "you" talking.

The problem is not that we have a mind, because we need one. The problem is that we tend to believe everything it says! After all, if it came from inside our heads, it must be true! Your mind will always whisper in your ear all the reasons why you should not be in love with your partner. It knows exactly what to tell you to keep you from intimacy. And it will pick it apart and pick it apart and pick it apart until there is nothing left to pick. And remember, this is the person you once idealized! So yes, your partner is a human being with all of their humanness and shortcomings and quirky habits—and so are you! They are also the person who still has all of the qualities that you fell in love with.

So the question becomes, why would you want to place your focus on all of the things that cause your relationship to depreciate? And what might happen if you shifted your attention to the things that you love and appreciate about your partner? Think of your attention as a beam of light that you can choose to shine onto anything you want. Imagine you are in a dark room and in one corner of the room is a treasure chest full of jewels and gold. In the other corner is a pile of dog shit. Where would you rather shine your light?

You can even think about your day today: how much of your time did you shine your light on the things you appreciate and how much of your time was focused on your complaints?

The ability to shift our awareness is a key factor in our ability to be happy as human beings.

"We are what we think. All that we are arises with our thoughts. With our thoughts, we make our world.
- Buddha

Appreciation is a Gift

Appreciation is a gift that we give to ourselves and to our partners. We are the beneficiaries of our own appreciation. The more we appreciate something the more we enjoy it. To appreciate is to become sensitively aware. For example, if we take an art appreciation course we learn to see more deeply into each piece of art. We become aware of the lines, the fine brushstrokes, the use of color and metaphor. We literally see things that go unnoticed by an untrained eye. If we take a music appreciation course, we learn to appreciate the different instruments, the subtle rhythms, the long lines of the melody and the nuances of the composition. The same is true in relationships. If you took a "relationship appreciation" course, you would begin to see more deeply into the subtleties of your partner, their qualities and character, the elements of their physical being, their emotional body and their spiritual essence. To complain is like having a god or goddess standing before you and choosing to focus on their cellulite instead of their magnificence. The very fact of you and your partner's existence is a miracle. How do you look at the miracles in your life?

Often the miracles in our lives, the things we love about a person, over time, become the things we take for granted. This is the result of seeing and relating to things in a habitual way. The tendency to form habitual ways of being and relating are inherent in our brain's agenda from millions of years of evolution. It likes to make habits out of things so it can ignore them and pay attention to the more important issues of survival, like lions springing out of the forest or foraging for food! Of course there aren't many lions in our life and foraging for food has become a trip to the grocery store or picking the tomatoes out of our garden. But the point is, habits can sometimes be useful. They help us organize our lives. However, habitual ways of seeing and relating can also be deadening and can suck the aliveness out of the relationship.

One of the best ways to get out of the "habit" with our partners is to instill a "practice of appreciation." A "practice" is something we do deliberately, a "habit" that pulls us out of our less productive tendencies. It's like learning to play the piano. Practice helps us to improve our proficiency. We can practice appreciation by finding one new thing each day to appreciate about our partners: "I really love the way you come home and sit down with the kids before dinner." "I really love the shape of your eyebrows." "Thank you for your willingness to help me with things around the house." "Thanks for just letting me just rest when I get home." "I appreciate your sense of humor—it always lifts my spirits."

These expressions not only offer positive reinforcement; they also let your partner know that what they do is really noticed and appreciated by you. This can have a profound transformational impact on your relationship over time. A practice of appreciation increases our awareness and makes us notice those subtleties that we may otherwise overlook.

John Gottman, the famous research psychologist on marriage, found that when people have a ratio of one to five (complaints about their partner to things they appreciate about their partner), they report having a happy marriage. As that ratio approaches more of a 1 to 1, people report feeling dissatisfied in their marriage. Once the scale tips the other way, Gottman is able to predict with a 97% rate of accuracy which couples will be divorced within a year! As a result of this, one couple I worked with took on a practice of keeping their appreciation ratio in the one to five category. So any time one of them complained to the other, such as "You didn't take out the garbage" or "You should dress up more," the other partner would look at them with a smile and say, "OK! Now gimme five!" And the complaining partner would offer five compliments or appreciations. They had fun with this activity and it really did keep the ratio in balance! Three months later they reported feeling much happier in their marriage.

Sometimes people think that they will lose something if they are appreciative. Nothing is further from the truth. You lose nothing and gain everything. People fear that it gives their partner an upper hand in the relationship. We fear that if we really value and appreciate we will lose control. Control of what? Do you think it is your job to control your partner? This is one of the mind games that keep us from true intimacy. But even if it were true, which would you rather be— happy or controlling? Notice that complaining does not make you—or your partner—happy!

Some people become very stingy with their appreciation. They dole it out in small increments if and when their partner does something that they want them to do. They make it completely conditional: "If you do what I want, you get a small dose of appreciation." They use it to control rather than love. Notice that you always have a choice for control or for love.

Generating Appreciation

Here's a 30-day assignment:

Each day this month, find something new to appreciate about your partner. For example, notice the shape of their eyes, the way they move their body, their perspective about things, or an element of their personality. Just keep finding something new. This will help you to develop the mental "muscle" that looks for appreciation rather than complaints. You'll begin to cultivate appreciation in yourself. It's like a garden that you water. If you water the seeds of appreciation you will experience your life as an ongoing flow of appreciation. If you water the seeds of complaint, you will experience you life as an ongoing flow of complaints. This is a choice.

Don't say anything critical for the 30 days, just acknowledge what you *do* like. Even if your partner forgets to take out the garbage you could say, "I really appreciate all of the things you do to help around here such as taking care of our cars and mowing the lawn. And thanks for picking up the groceries on the way home."

See what happens when you infuse your relationship with the spirit of appreciation instead of complaint!

Answer these questions:

My partner likes to be acknowledged for…

Examples:

> *Something she has done*
> *Her qualities and character*
> *Her looks*
> *Other*

I like to be acknowledged for…

> *Something I've done*
> *My personal qualities and character*
> *My looks*
> *Other*

Although we all like to be acknowledged and appreciated, most people are not very good at the skills of giving and receiving appreciation. Try these suggestions.

How to Give a "High Powered" Appreciation

When giving appreciation, it is good to know what your partner most likes to be appreciated for. The above are examples of the kinds of things we appreciate about each other. When you offer an appreciation make sure of the following:

1. <u>You have the person's full attention</u> so that they can fully hear and receive the appreciation and not just brush it off. Many people are somewhat uncomfortable receiving appreciations and will easily dismiss them or not even hear them. In my work with one couple, the husband acknowledged his wife for something she had done during our discussion, and when I mentioned it later, she hadn't even heard the acknowledgement! So make sure your partner hears you by making eye contact; you can even ask them to tell you what they heard you say to make sure it "registered."

2. <u>Tell them in detail what you appreciate</u>. Not just, "Hey you did a good job!" But, " I really appreciate the way you went out of your way to get all the ingredients for this dinner and that you put so much love and care into making it. I could taste it in every delicious bite!"

3. <u>Then tell them why you appreciate it</u>, and what it does for you. For example: "It really makes me feel special and cared for that you would take the time to make me such a wonderful meal."

In receiving appreciation, avoid any form of dismissal: "Oh it was nothing" or "It's no big deal." Dismissing or not really taking in someone's appreciation of you is like being given a very special gift and throwing it in the trash right in front of the giver. It hurts! When we appreciate someone we really want our thanks and appreciation to be received. An appropriate response is: "Thank you for noticing." Or, "You're welcome!" Notice if you are uncomfortable with it and just be curious about your own discomfort. Open up to being appreciated. No need to do anything else with it.

In addition to verbally expressing appreciation there are other ways to show it:

Answer these questions:

Little things/small gestures that my partner appreciates are...

Examples:

> *Holding their hand*
> *Bringing them a flower or card*
> *Saying something nice about them*
> *Washing the dishes or some other work around the house*
> *Other*

My partner feels significant or important to me when I...

Examples:

> *Tell them they are...*
> *Do something to take care of them*
> *Hold them, kiss them*
> *Notice something about them*
> *Other*

It makes me feel important when they...

Examples:

> *Tell me I am special*
> *Do something to take care of me*
> *Hug and kiss me*
> *Notice something good about me and tell me*
> *Other*

What makes you feel important?

Again, share your answers with your partner. Ask them how they might answer some of these questions. It's a great way to open up an interesting and informative dialogue and it will deepen your relationship as you answer honestly and express genuine interest in your partner's answers.

7

Communication:
The Number One Most Significant
Factor in Successful Relationships

Couples who are able to communicate openly and in healthy ways about the things that matter to them report greater closeness and intimacy in their relationships. The more people are able to share about themselves—who they are, the truth about their wants and desires, expectations and disappointments, thoughts and feelings—the more intimacy and depth they experience with one another. Communication is the heart of relationship. The ability to communicate successfully is the number one most significant factor in the success of both personal and professional relationships. Developing this skill is key to a happy and successful marriage. In addition to the "skill" of speaking is the factor of "realness" or authenticity. How real do we get with each other? What is our level of openness and honesty? In this next section you will look at your ideas about communication in marriage. I will offer you suggestions for communicating and resources for developing your own communication skills. Let's start by looking at the subject of intimacy. Are you willing to get real in your relationship and let your partner know who you really are?

Taking it Deeper

As a couples coach, one of the questions I am often asked is "How do I create more intimacy and closeness in my relationship?"

Intimacy in relationships is largely about revealing. In other words, the more you reveal about who you really are, the more intimate the relationship becomes. The more you reveal about all aspects of yourself the more you feel loved for who you are in the relationship. Revealing is the dropping of the personas or "masks" that we wear with each other. In other words, we let go of trying to "maintain our image" with our partner. We fear doing this because we doubt our own lovability. We believe that we may not be as lovable as the image we wish to project. We can't commit to always love someone "no matter what" as love is an organic experience—we either feel it or we don't. We don't "decide" to fall in love and we don't "decide" to fall out of love. But we can begin to understand the factors that generate the experience of love. For example, we don't decide to love, but we can decide to be personally honest and transparent. When I am personally honest with myself and with you, we have the basis for a real relationship—a relationship built on a solid base of truthfulness. It isn't always "pleasant," but it is always real. And when you love me, I know that it is really me you love because I have been transparent with you.

Over the years I've noticed that couples who reveal themselves to each other experience greater levels of intimacy despite disagreements. They become less judgmental and more accepting of each other's differences and preferences. Less revealing couples create a certain subtle distancing that inhibits deeper intimacy. Sometimes this distance is not so subtle but is a tall wall behind which each person stand, peering over the top at their partner. Our relationships may be more compatible on the surface because we don't tell our partners anything that might create friction. However, in the absence of disclosure, we are left with our "stories" about our partner. By stories, I mean the thoughts and ideas that play in our heads about them. From behind our tall wall, we project our own ideas, fears and fantasies onto our partner. We imagine we know what they are "really thinking." Instead of having more truthfulness and understanding of our partners, we have our "story about them and they have their story about us"

As author Byron Katie says, "We have our story about people and they have their story about us and no two people have ever met!" When we hide things about ourselves from our partners, we affirm to ourselves that there is something wrong with the way we think and feel. And that makes it harder to believe they really love "us" because, well…they don't really know us. It compounds any sense of deficiency that we may already feel about ourselves. Being honest about how you really feel and think allows your partner to know you and to love the real you with all your humanness, not some image you need to maintain.

The truth is a powerful medicine that has a healing affect on the relationship and on both people. It can also sometimes shake things up and wake us up to what is really going on! It can also be a potent aphrodisiac. I can tell you from my own experience of having to hear—and deliver—some very tough truths in my life that it always takes us where we need to go. We can see this in hindsight. You can think about the difficult truths you've told in your life and ultimately where it led you - to where you are today. There is enormous freedom in the truth. We stop protecting ourselves and instead open up to the flow of the universe as it unfolds around what is real and true. It opens up channels of energy between couples and breathes fresh air into the system.

Truth Telling

When I work with couples, especially couples who complain that they have "grown apart" or "have lost that lovin' feeling," one of the first things I ask is, "Is there anything that you have not told the complete truth about?" This is a scary question. Because most couples have lots of things that they haven't really told the truth about. One couple I worked with had been married for twenty-five years. They were like a pair of shoes—comfortable with each other, used to each other. But there was a noticeable lack of vitality in both of them and in the relationship. As we continued to work together we discovered that she had been angry at him for twenty-five years because he had flirted with another women during their honeymoon! She had never said anything about it, but she had closed her heart at that moment and had never fully opened it again. As this was disclosed in our work together, something amazing happened. They began to talk about all kinds of things they'd never discussed and they became more affectionate and close. By the end of the week they looked like two people on their honeymoon!

This is the power of disclosure. When we come into the truth with each other and say the things that need to be said, vitality is restored and intimacy is opened up.

Part One: Expectations & Assumptions

Answer these questions:

What are your expectations of yourself regarding honest communication in your relationship?

What are your expectations of your partner regarding honesty in communication?

Are you a good listener?

What are the things you most fear sharing and opening up about?

How would you like your partner to let you know when there is something you do that bothers or upsets them? In other words, what is the best way for your intimate partner to give you feedback?

What is it that someone should never do in giving you feedback?

How often do you take time to "check in" about how you each are feeling about your lives and about the relationship?

What do you most appreciate about the way your partner communicates?

> *What bothers you most about the way your partner communicates?*
> *What do you assume your partner's answers would be to these questions?*

One of the primary reasons that people fear telling the truth is that they don't know what will happen when they do, and they fear negative consequences such as hurting or disappointing their partners, looking bad, or the possibility that the relationship could end. Therefore, we attempt to control the other person's feelings and choices through withholding information from them. On some level, all withholding of truth is a control trip. We want the other person to feel and think and do what WE want—rather than what is real or true for them.

When we tell them our truth, we "risk" that they will feel and act differently than we want them to. The choice for open and honest communication is a choice for an authentic, real relationship, rather than a relationship we control. In choosing authenticity, we step into a higher game—one where we give up the illusion of a "guarantee" or the attempt to manipulate our partner.. We choose instead to have a real relationship, with real truth, real responses, real consequences and real rewards. The quality of a relationship connection based on truth is very different than one based on manipulation. Every communication is a choice for either control or authenticity.

Answer these questions for yourself:

> *Is there something you haven't told your partner the truth about? This could be something about your past, something you have done, something you think or feel, something you want, something that bothers you or anything else. Is there anything you are afraid they might "find out" about you? What is your fear in telling your partner? What is the worst thing that could happen?*
> *Is there any other possibility? What is the best that could happen?*
> *What do you think would actually happen? What is your most realistic assessment?*
> *What are the costs of not telling the truth in your relationship?*

If you are withholding secrets or lies, there is already a psychic wall that is up between you and your partner. It's hard for us to really feel loved and cherished by someone when we believe that they don't really know the whole story of who we are. When we can reveal ourselves in all of our glory and with all of our shortcomings, mistakes, and lessons we've learned, we reveal ourselves as a whole human being. As a friend of mine used to say, "Every saint has a past and every sinner has a future." We can forgive and be forgiven. I usually recommend trusting the truth. As they say, "The truth shall set you free." However, it may first freak you out a bit. We must be willing to trust our partners with the truth of who we are. And to be present and understanding of their fears and reactions.

When my ex-husband revealed to me that he had had an affair, it wasn't the end of our relationship. It was actually the beginning of a new conversation based on reality and an updating of who we were at that time. It became clear that we each had things we were afraid to share in fear of rocking the boat and possibly losing what we had. Which is always a possibility and which is what eventually happened in the end. But had we had those conversations earlier, there is a good possibility that we would have been able to work out our dissatisfactions and avoided the affair. Or discovered that our relationship was not working for one or both of us and resolved it or moved on. I have found this to be the case with many couples I've worked with. People who "drift" from their commitment and begin to move their eros outside of the relationship usually have communication issues they need to work out inside of their relationship. More on this in the section on sex.

While having the courage to engage in open and honest communication is crucial in relationships, it is best to be able to do it skillfully. In this next section I will teach you how to tell the truth in a way that stops arguments and creates more closeness and connection.

Skills: On Truth Telling

Think about these questions and answer them honestly for yourself.

Establishing Intention. What is the purpose of your communication? What do you want to have happen as a result of this communication?

- What do you want for yourself?
- What do you want for your partner?
- What do you want for the relationship?

The No-Blame, Inarguable Truth

The idea of the truth being something inarguable was first introduced to me by Drs.Gay and Kathlyn Hendricks. I loved the way it simplified communication and find it a useful, easily accessible tool for communicating.

Basically, th1ere are two different kinds of statements that someone can make: Those that can be argued, and those that are inarguable. The problem most people have is that they tend to make highly arguable statements as if they were inarguably true. As a result, we find ourselves in all kinds of arguments. When we learn the difference between arguable and inarguable communication we have the ability to stop arguments in their tracks and productively resolve our differences. Below are some examples of the difference between arguable and inarguable statements. Notice that inarguable statements are things that you say about yourself: your experience, your wants, desires, feeling, physicality, etc. It can also include facts such as "the temperature is eighty degrees." Statements that involve memory are arguable. We know that people remember things differently and we've all had the experience of "remembering" something we were quite sure about, and then discovering it really wasn't accurate after all. Overall, memory is a bad test for reality. Conversations about who said what and things of that nature tend to illicit arguments and are generally unproductive. There is a big difference between saying: "What I thought I heard you say is…" and "You said…"

Our responses are generated by what we "hear," not what is "said." Since we all interpret words, gestures and facial expressions a little differently, we often bring very different meanings to each others' communications.

We often misinterpret or mishear someone's communication and so it is always best to check at the time to see if we are on the same page. A large percentage of arguments in relationships are caused by broken agreements, and many of those were misunderstandings of what the agreement actually was! So clarifying agreements and reliably keeping them is very, very important if you want to avoid arguments.

Arguable	Inarguable
You shouldn't do that.	I get scared when you do that.
You said	What I heard is....
It's good that you did that.	I feel happy that you did that
What really happened is	What I remember is

The next time you find yourself arguing with someone, pay attention to your arguable statements. See if you can shift the conversation by changing your statement to something inarguable. For example: "Its too hot in here" is arguable. "I feel too hot" is unarguable.

3. Resolving a Relationship Problem Worksheet

To be responsible as a speaker is to see yourself as the source of your own experience in the relationship. It is not to see yourself as a victim, but as a participant in every relationship interaction. Our interactions and the way we jointly "show up" create the experience of the relationship. It is the hand drawing the hand in the MC Escher piece "Drawing Hands":

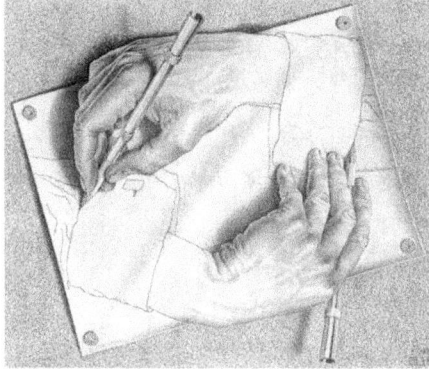

We each generate responses in each other through our behaviors, actions, speaking and listening. When we put our attention on our own part in all matters we empower ourselves to create the relationship we want. When we can own our part in any issue, we take back control over our own happiness. This opens up new possibilities for feeling and action.

Use the following worksheet to work through any relationship drama or issue that arises.

Resolving a Relationship Problem

1. Tell the No-Blame, Inarguable Truth

Talk about what you saw, heard and felt without judging or analyzing. Just observations, no accusations, no dramatizing or minimizing.

Example: For the last week I notice that you've broken your agreement with me three times to be home for dinner.

2. Describe your personal feelings

What emotions do you experience around this issue? Note: Emotions are words like scared, upset, frustrated, mad, sad, glad. It can also be physical: I feel a lump in my throat, a knot in my stomach, I find it hard to breathe. It's like "reporting" to your partner how you experience the issue. It is not your analysis of the situation or your opinions.

Example: I feel sad and hurt and I'm worried about why this may be happening. Tonight I got really angry about it.

3. Own your part in the issue

Take responsibility for being part of the dynamic that is creating the issue. Clue: If the issue is in your life and in your marriage, it has something to do with you. It doesn't exist independently of you. See if you can find anything that you do or don't do, that contributes to a situation. That is not the same as blaming yourself. It is just stepping up to the plate, seeing your part, and choosing to relate to any problem from a stance of personal responsibility.

Example: "I realize that I've also broken an agreement I had with you. Also, instead of saying anything to you about your being late, before I've just acted like it was OK, which may have given you the message that it didn't bother me, leading to your being late again." (Note: You are really looking with interest and curiosity about how you may have contributed to the dynamic.)

4. Ask your partner what their experience is.

Listen. Clarify. Reserve judgment.

*Example: How do **you** see this and how do you feel about what I said?*

5. Continue in this way until there is clarity for both of you.

6. What requests would you like to make of your partner?

What agreements can you make going forward that will help resolve this?

Example: I realize that from time to time something may make you late. However, I would like to request that you keep your agreement with me to be on time. If there is an urgent situation, I'd like you to call me as soon as you know so that I am not here waiting and worrying.

One possibility is to write down on a sheet of paper all of your ideas and all of their ideas. Then cross off any that are completely unacceptable to either of you. Discuss the ones remaining and create your agreements about them.

7. Recommit to your relationship together and to resolving anything that gets in the way of being close.

Tips:

Avoid statements that generate arguments:

Judgments, analyzing, criticizing

"Shoulding" (Anything that starts with "You should or shouldn't..." After all, how would you know what they should or shouldn't do with their life?)

Making them "wrong" or "bad" as a person

Assuming you know things that you don't, such as what they are "really" thinking or doing.

Blaming, accusing

Assuming that you've got "the whole picture" and they are "clueless"

Trying to get them to "admit" they are wrong or bad

Getting stuck on petty points or technicalities, such as "who said what." Most of the time people remember these things differently. And many times what we thought someone said is not what they said. So speak about "what I heard" or "my understanding was" rather than "what you said." It's a more truthful statement and it's unarguable.

Defending, rationalizing

Throw a tantrum, get dramatic

Instead, tell the No-Blame Truth:

The No-Blame truth turns an argument into a real conversation!

Stick with: "I" statements, feelings, observations, requests, personal responsibility (your part).

"I" Statements:

I feel, I believe, I want, I saw, I hear, I like, I don't like, I wish, I assumed, I did, I didn't, etc.

Avoid following any of these openers with the word "you" (example: I feel YOU are a jerk! I want YOU to get YOUR act together!). That is just an arguable statement in disguise as an I statement. Instead: I feel sad. I want to be able to trust what you tell me.

What are your interpretations/meanings about this? (It is important to note that your interpretations are different from the facts.) These are all the thoughts in your head about it. The primary difference between facts and thoughts is that one exists in reality (objective) and the other is made up (subjective). When we are upset about something it is not the facts but **what we believe the facts mean**. Example: You were late, so that means you don't care about me. Late may be a fact, but the meaning is subjective. We tend to think our interpretations are facts. They aren't. All upsets in relationship exist in the meanings that we assign to behaviors and action. The meanings that we assign tend to be repetitive: I can't trust them, They are bad, I am bad, I'm right, they're wrong, they're just trying to ....). See if you can identify the underlying interpretations that are stress producing. Share your interpretations as interpretations, but find out what is really true by asking and discussion.

Question your interpretations!

8

Turn Your Complaints into Requests

What is your primary "complaint" about your partner (or if you currently have no complaints, what about the last relationship?) For example:

a. They don't do enough

b. They don't really appreciate me or are too critical

c. They never give me anything

d. They aren't available enough

e. They aren't affectionate enough

What is your partner's biggest complaint about you? (Or what was their complaint about their prior relationship?) Here is a secret you need to know that will change the way you hear complaints forever: Complaints are requests in disguise!

Complaints reveal the requests we are not making. These are things we want but rather than be vulnerable and ask for them, we complain instead! The opportunity in hearing a complaint is to identify the underlying request. Our complaints show us what our values are, what matters to us, what we care about.

Of course complaining is a very unpleasant form of speaking and ideally we can shift this way of speaking to something more productive by doing one thing: turn all complaints into direct requests.

Listen to your own complaints before they come out of your mouth and hear the underlying request. What might happen if you just ask for what you want instead of complaining about what you don't have?

What requests do you have for your partner? For example:

Do more household chores

Be more appreciative, less negative

Remember birthdays, anniversaries, and give me a gift

Spend time with me, go away with me

Be more physical in the relationship

Can you offer specific examples of what you mean?

What requests does your partner make of you? Or what requests can you hear underneath their complaints?

The more you are able to turn complaints into direct requests, the more likely you are of getting what you actually want! A request sounds like this:

"Will you do _____ for me this week? I would love that."
"Would you be willing to _____ for me tonight?"

Those are direct requests. Notice that the following are not:

"I don't suppose you'd want to…"

"If you really loved me you would…"

"Can you…" *(Can is a question that asks about capability rather than action.)*

Notice also, what you do to avoid a direct request. For example:

Hint, imply, withdraw, be punitive, act like everything is fine when it's not, minimize the importance of what you want ("oh it's nothing really…"), get dramatic, throw a tantrum, criticize, complain, be sarcastic, joke about it, etc. In short, anything to avoid asking the question. The reason we are loath to just ask is because asking makes us vulnerable!

If we ask, they may say no! Or worse, they may say yes! Notice if you have certain "hidden rules" like "it doesn't count if I have to ask you to do it." Rules like this are a set-up for failure. The reason is that the other person can't read our minds or "know" what we want. This is especially true for women who have the expectation that men should just know what we want. They don't… Generally, men would love to give women what they want if they could just find out what the heck it is! But since women don't like to say, it puts us all in an impossible position. Get over your idea that they should just know. It is really a child's idea, based on the need we had for our parents to just "know" what we needed before we were old enough to formulate the thought and even afterward.

Often, we try to recreate the same sense of "being taken care of" that we had as children by wanting our partner to just know what we need all the time and by wanting them to always think of us before themselves. These are the expectations that need to be updated from childhood. Our partner is not our parent. We need to meet in the relationship as adults who have the capacity to meet many of our own needs and who can ask our partner for the things we want from them. We need to meet as adults who are capable of hearing and accepting someone's "no." We must finally accept the fact that our partner's life does not completely revolve around us, and that they have their own needs, limitations, desires and boundaries to consider. When we make a request we are asking our partner to consider our needs along with their own—not instead of their own. It is unreasonable to expect our partner to always give us what we want or do what we ask.

Let's talk about an appropriate response to a request. Again, a request to your partner does not mean that they have to do it, or that if they don't do it, they don't love you. There are many reasons why a person cannot fulfill a request. Again, we have an opportunity to drop our childlike expectation that someone should fulfill our every request. A real request has room for a "no", without punishment. There are actually three possible responses to a request:

1. *Yes*

2. *No*

3. *A counter-offer*

A counter-offer or negotiation

Sometimes we cannot or do not wish to fulfill a request, but we can offer an alternative in the same spirit that may fulfill the underlying desire of our partner. Often, the thing we ask for is something we want because it will make us feel better. Our partner may offer something that can fulfill the desire but in a different way or perhaps at a different time. Be open to possibilities. There is usually more than one way to get what we want or need. Don't turn it into a power struggle. Instead, find out what you both want in any situation, and then see if there is someway that both of those things can happen. For example, you may want your spouse to help clean and they may want to relax. Perhaps you can come up with a schedule where both of those things can be accomplished.

Avoid the "either/or" mentality: your way or my way. There are more than one or two possibilities in the universe and when you can let go of polarizing your positions, you can usually find an option that will accomplish what is needed or create an alternative that is better than either idea. Look at the following diagram. Notice that the two lines coming from the bottom L and R points of the triangle meet at a point in the middle above the two of them. Normally, we "compromise". In other words we find something that is half-way between your idea and mine and neither of us are really happy about it. The new idea is to find a third way of doing something that is a higher idea then either of the two positions.

C. The Better Idea

A. Your idea   B. My idea

Compromise

Look for the better idea that neither of you have thought of yet. Compromising may just indicate a lack of creativity. Think outside the box for solutions. Don't hold your position just to be right. You may be able to "get" your partner to do something but at what cost? Generally you will end up with someone who feels resentful. Instead, find what can work for both of you without giving up what you need. Instead of thinking it has to be "A" (my way) or "B" (your way), think A plus B. How can we both get what we need here? Look for the deeper desire under the request.

Question your strategy!

9
The Power of Listening

"The first duty of love is to listen."
- Paul Tillich, American theologian
and philosopher

"Deep listening is miraculous for both listener and speaker. When someone receives us with open-hearted, non-judging, intensely interested listening, our spirits expand."
- Sue Patton Thoele

Most discussion on communication centers around speaking. We think about what we want to say, who we want to say it to, how we want to say it, what our intention is. We often prepare for a speech, a conversation or a meeting where we need to present ideas and information. But how often do you "prepare" to listen? How often do you think about the quality of your listening, or even ask yourself the question, "**How** do I want to listen?"

Yet listening is probably the most important part of communication. After all, if no one is listening, why bother to say anything? The way we listen can give someone the experience of being heard or it can give someone the experience of being judged, analyzed, "fixed," dismissed or a host of other experiences. In the listening model I want to introduce you to, you will learn how to deeply hear into another person's communication. This will take you beyond the spoken word, to the essence of what they are saying and feeling. You will learn to let go of judgment and biases that you have about the other person and be present to them and to their communication.

When we are truly listened to, something transformational happens. Our spirits soar. We feel like someone really gets who we are. We matter. We exist in the listening of the other. We come into being through the quality of their listening. We hear ourselves. We take our place in the relationship. Listening is one of the greatest gifts you can offer your partner throughout your entire marriage. It often creates an enormous sense of relief and many times is actually all that may be needed to resolve a problem.

In order to listen fully we need to become aware of what impedes listening. Every human being has his or her own unique listening style. We each have our own built-in listening filters and tendencies, through which we screen what is being said. This is an "automatic" way of listening that we have developed over many years. We automatically hear things a certain way. When you listen to another person speak, you are simultaneously listening to their words, tone, inflection, volume, body language and facial expression. Our brain gathers up all of these bits of information and interprets them into a specific meaning and intent.

There are three aspects to a communication:

1. Content

2. Presentation

3. Intent

Notice that the first two are the audio-visual portion of the program. You hear and see content and presentation with your ears and eyes. It is the "what" and the "how" of the communication – what is being said and how is it being stated? However the third part, intent, is the **invisible** part of the communication. It is from the content and presentation that we interpret the **meaning and intent** of the speaker.

However, the meaning that we assign to the communication is the result of our own mental processes and conditioning, based upon a lifetime of reactions to specific words, voice intonation, pitch, volume and gestures. From all of this we assign **our** meaning to **their** communication. In other words, "This is what **I** mean by what you said." In other words, this is the meaning I assume. Rarely do we check to see if what we heard or understood is related to what they said, or what they meant by what they said.

Our listening filters live in our blind spot.

In business, for example, often the nuances of our listening filters are related to our job responsibilities. A CFO might screen other people's ideas through a listening filter of financial feasibility. Meanwhile, the head of human resources might screen the same information through a filter of what it is going to take to train new employees. The sales person listens for opportunities to close the sale. In the same way that you employ your professional listening filters at work, there is a whole range of other listening filters engaged in the background of our unconscious. For example you may have an automatic listening for whether people like you or not. You may hear communications as accusations or criticism. You may have an automatic listening for "What do I need to fix?" or "What do they want from me?" We don't notice that these are our interpretations, we just assume that this is, in fact, what they really mean!

Examples:

Speaker: I don't think your idea will work.

Listener interpretation: You don't like me or my ideas. You think I'm stupid.

Speaker: We need to hurry if we are going to be on time.

Listener interpretation: Oh, so you think I'm too slow. I guess, what you want is more important then what I want.

Speaker: I think that's a good idea.

Listener interpretation: Great! I can go ahead and do it.

Speaker: I appreciate what you did.

Listener interpretation: Flattery...what does he want from me now?

We selectively listen for the information our filters are seeking. We seek "evidence" to support a pre-determined perception: They like me, they don't like me, they think I'm right, they think I'm wrong, I'm smart, I'm stupid, I have to do it all myself, they don't trust me, they won't support my idea, they're just trying to get something out of me, I'm being criticized, etc.

Listening Filters and Speaking Biases

Your listening biases are also linked to your speaking biases and affect how you present your ideas. For instance, if your filter is focused on criticism, you might present your ideas in a defensive way. You might anticipate being criticized, and rebut objections before they are even voiced. If your filter is focused on wanting acceptance you might offer to do things that you really don't want to do and end up feeling overloaded or resentful.

Listening filters and speaking biases are habits that we have developed over time. Like all habits, some are useful and some are not. When we consciously employ a style of listening for a particular purpose, we can use our filters beneficially. When we don't even notice that we are listening a certain way and interpreting meanings from these filters, it can often cause problems in communication.

Handling the Special Challenges of Stress

During any significant challenge that generates stress, or when we are faced with personal obstacles, we tend to fall into our automatic ways of listening, speaking and responding. Effective communicators are familiar with their filters and biases and habitual ways of hearing and speaking. They know how to employ new ways of thinking, listening, speaking and acting in order to create different results.

I will now give you some skills that you can utilize and practice with your partner. The original model was introduced to me by my friend and colleague Ron Bynum. He adapted the model from a book called How To Listen So Kids Will Talk, How to Talk So Kids Will Listen, by Adele Farber and shaped it for business people. I have made some changes in the model to make it more accessible and user-friendly for couples.

I highly recommend practicing generous listening every chance you get until you begin to do it naturally as an automatic part of the way you listen to your partner. It will open up communication in your relationship more than anything else I can recommend. Generous listening makes it safe for the other person to communicate because they know you are listening for the best in them and they experience feeling "heard" at a deep level. Many times people are not even aware of their own honorable intent until we point it out! Once honorable intent is understood and is on the table, you'll find it easier to discuss options, ideas, and strategies with your partner. When people feel heard, they generally respond in kind by becoming better listeners themselves.

Generous Listening

"We do not see things as they are, we see them as we are.
We do not hear things as they are, we hear them as we are."
- Anais Nin

What It Is:

Generous listening is listening with a deep appreciation of the feelings, reality and needs of another, contributing to the other person's experience of being understood. It is "generous" because it requires momentarily putting aside your own biases and needs.

The premise of generous listening is that every communication has behind it an honorable intention or an unspoken concern. This honorable intent or unspoken concern may or may not be well articulated, and may or may not be something you personally agree with. In listening generously, we listen ultimately for that honorable "nugget of gold." Listening for the honorable intent of the speaker forwards the communication toward harmonic reso- lution and collaborative action. The honorable intent is generally something that is "supportable." For example, someone's honor- able intent may be to do something good, but you may not nec- essarily agree with what that is or how to do it. But we honor the desire to do something good or well meaning. When you can name and give voice to the honorable intent or unseen concern, some- thing absolutely astonishing occurs. The speaker will generally be blown away by how fully you grasp the essence of their intent and concerns. They feel deeply understood and think "Wow! You really GET it!" This level of hearing is a gift. It offers the possibility of a true resolution. Surprisingly, the speaker often does not recognize their own honorable intent or unspoken concern. They are generally speaking over or around it. So when you can listen for it and name it for them, it usually takes them by surprise (in a very good way!) and opens them up to you.

3 Positive Results:

Generous listening will take both people to the heart of a communication. When done effectively, three positive results will occur:

The listener will fully understand the speaker's point of view.
The speaker will feel fully heard, understood and appreciated.
The listener and the speaker will both open up to new possibilities and creative solutions to the problem or issue at hand.

Steps to Generous Listening

1. Offer Your Undivided Attention

Show that you are fully there, fully attentive to the message you are receiving. Maintain positive eye contact. Show the speaker that you are hearing the message being sent. Show that you are not only available but also actively engaged in receiving the message. No multi-tasking! Be fully present. Resist the urge to make comments or to judge anything being said. Just listen. Don't interrupt. You'll get to talk later.

2. Paraphrase It Back

Repeat back what you heard with a minimum of interpretation. Show that you understand the content of what is being said. You don't need to "parrot" what they say word for word as this tends to sound awkward or annoying, just make sure you really have the basic content of the message and its meaning. Clarify anything about the message to ensure understanding. For example: "So what I'm hearing is …" (paraphrase without interpreting) or "Let me make sure that I am understanding you correctly…" Let them correct any misunderstanding or interpretation. Paraphrasing allows us to make sure that we are actually hearing correctly (which we often don't) and understand what they mean by what they are saying (which we often don't.)

3. Name the Feeling

Demonstrate that you empathize with the human emotion the speaker is experiencing. This will build bridges of rapport. When you name a feeling use an "emotion" word. Don't use concepts or analysis. Don't judge what they are saying. Just hear the underlying dominant emotion that is present in their voice and body language and mirror that back to them so they get that you really understand how they are feeling. For example: "It sounds as if you're feeling a little frustrated about this," or, "If I were you I'd probably be feeling pretty angry." or, "You must be so disappointed about that!" Match their level of emotional intensity with the appropriate word. For example, are they feeling "annoyed" or "furious?" Both may be levels of intensity of anger, but one is just slight, while the other is intense. Don't minimize or dramatize their feeling, just see if you can identify it where it is.

4. Recognize the honorable intention and unspoken concern of the speaker

Listen for the honorable, supportable intent. The speaker is communicating that there is something he/she really cares about. Listen for that concern, the underlying needs or values of the speaker. Acknowledging what really matters to him/her encourages the speaker to move toward a positive, purposeful resolution.

Example: "I hear how important it is to you that…"

"I appreciate how much you really care about..."

"I really understand your frustration with this and how much you want…"

This generally has a profound impact on the speaker.. If you "miss" it, don't worry; this can give the speaker the opportunity to clarify what they really want and what matters most to them. It is not crucial that you "get it right" the first time, but that you are **trying** to and that opens up a conversation that allows the clarity to emerge. Keep going for it until you find it.

Once we get the person's intent and align with it we can negotiate possibilities and strategies that work for both of us. Often times we confuse strategy with intent. It's important to separate those two in order to "get" the intent. Then collaborate on strategy.

Ex:: Strategy: I want to go out to dinner with you.

Possible Underlying Intent: I want to have a quiet, intimate evening enjoying each other's company.

New strategies may or may not involve dinner or even going out. Just find out why the person wants to do what they want and it will point to the underlying intent. Then come up with other ways to fulfill it if you don't want to go out to dinner.

Question your own listening!

10
The Drama Triangle

In every relationship "drama" there is a certain dynamic in place. This dynamic can be found between individuals, groups of people and even nations. It's something that we can even do by ourselves within our own minds. The triangle consists of three or more people taking on one of three roles:

The Victim

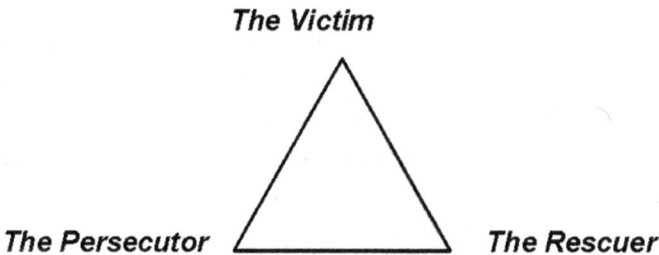

The Persecutor   **The Rescuer**

A friend of mine who is a therapist also playfully refers to this as:

"Oh no! I'm screwed!" (victim)

"Poor you! You're screwed!" (rescuer)

"Screw You!" (persecutor)

The Players:

The Victim

The victim is the person who feels used, abused or taken advantage of in some way. Often they are, but they don't see their own part in the dynamic. Generally, it's in their blind spot. They believe something is being "done to them." They tend to see themselves as helpless and are not in touch with (or conscious of) the choices they have made—or can now make—that keep them in the victim role. They generally are blaming the persecutor."

The Persecutor

Often people who have felt victimized become persecutors. They've reached their limit and now want to retaliate or get even. They still see themselves as a victim on some level. They often have a complaint about the victim or the rescuer. They blame them for why they have the right to be the persecutor.

The Rescuer

The rescuer is usually someone who sees the predicament of the victim, buys into their helplessness, and wants to "save" them from the persecutor. They see themselves as empowered to help resolve the problem since the victim can't. It is a one up/one down perspective, as are the other two roles. It is not a perspective in which we see people as equals. Rescuers eventually become martyrs who then feel like victims because they "take care of everyone but themselves." They blame the victim and the persecutor.

A Culture Of Blame

The Drama Triangle is a culture of blame. Blaming someone is what puts us on the triangle.

Generally these roles play out in families (mom, dad, kid) with people rotating their positions on the triangle. The problem is that all of these roles arise out of blame. We blame the other person for our problem. We do not take personal responsibility for ourselves or allow others to do the same. We take more than our share of responsibility or less than our share and end up in one of these roles. When we can own our part and relate to whatever is occurring from a stance of responsibility, we can make choices that take us off the triangle. We take the perspective that is most empowering for all involved.

Here's how the dynamic works: Imagine the triangle as three separate people. Think of a particular drama that shows up in your own family from time to time. Perhaps dad is the persecutor. The persecutor is generally the designated "bad guy" in the dynamic. Perhaps he is angry with his kid. The kid is getting yelled at and feels attacked in some way by dad. In this case, the kid is the designated victim. Then here comes mom, who sees dad persecuting her child. She gets angry at dad for beating up on the kid and becomes the rescuer.

Sound familiar? This is a classic scene. Something along these lines goes on in all families, work places and even between groups of people and whole countries. But it goes on from there:

From dad's perspective, perhaps the kid did something he felt was disrespectful. In that case dad actually feels victimized by the kid! When mom jumps all over him, he feels even more victimized. So although dad may appear to be the persecutor, in his own mind he may see himself as the victim and both the kid and mom as persecutors.

But wait, there's more! Let's move this to the workplace. Let's say an employee is being chewed out by a manager for not doing his job. After the reprimand, another employee comes up to sympathize and agrees that the boss is a jerk. Sound familiar? The two of them then go around bad mouthing the boss. People begin to pull their support from the boss. Who is the victim now? Who are the persecutors? You see how the roles change? What happens is this:

Each of the positions on the triangle have an accompanying emotional component. For example, think about a time either in the past or currently, when you felt victimized. What were the feelings you experienced? How about a time when you rescued someone, or took their side? How about a time when you chewed someone out or pulled your support? People generally describe these feelings:

Victim: Sad, scared, helpless, hopeless, powerless, angry

Rescuer: Good, sympathetic, tired, exhausted, burdened, resentful

Persecutor: Righteous, indignant, angry, and later... guilty!

Notice that the rescuer may start out feeling like the "good guy." Those who keep on rescuing, eventually feel burdened, martyred and taken advantage of. Notice the shift from rescuer to victim here. People who keep rescuing often end up feeling resentful about constantly taking care of others. So at some point rescuers end up feeling used or like a victim themselves. Notice the emotional progression with victims. As we saw above, a persecutor is someone who felt victimized and then attacked back or "got even."

In other words, people keep moving around the triangle. But if you speak with anyone on the triangle, most of the time they see themselves as the victim. In fact, relationship dramas are really a race for the victim position! We love to see ourselves as the victim! In fact this is usually the problem—everyone thinks they are the victims of everyone else. If you pick up a newspaper you can see this among groups of people and among nations. Everyone thinks they are the ones being victimized and that everyone else is taking advantage of them or is out to get them. People who are on the attack are generally doing so because they feel they have been victimized. So the issue is really an issue of responsibility.

To recap: The way onto the triangle is through blame. The way off of the triangle is through personal responsibility.

Question your "blaming!"

11
Personal Responsibility

"No matter how much you point the finger and blame someone it will never change anything about you."
- Wayne Dyer

Responsibility does not mean blame, shame or guilt. Responsibility is a choice. It is the way that we choose to relate to the circumstances of our life. We see ourselves as the cause of our life and our experience. From that perspective we can make choices for change. Without that perspective we see ourselves as helpless and at the effect of people and circumstances. In any given situation, we are either taking responsibility or we are not.

"Deep change requires more than the identification of the problem and a call for action. It requires looking beyond the scope of the problem and finding the actual source of the trouble. The real problem is frequently located where we would least expect to find it, inside ourselves."
- Robert E. Quinn, Deep Change

What is Responsibility?

One of the hallmarks of personal maturity has to do with our relationship to responsibility, freedom and choice. As newborn infants, all choices are made for us. As we develop, we come into greater and greater relationship with choice. We make choices about how we think and act, where we go, what we do, what we say, how we say it, what we eat, who our friends are, where we work, where we live, and so forth. We make choices every day. The choices we have made in our past have resulted in our present circumstances. The choices we make today are creating our future.

When we were young our parents often attempted to teach us responsibility by devising rewards and punishments for "responsible behavior" or for failing to "act responsibly." As a result, many of us think responsibility is a synonym for burden, blame, fault, shame or guilt For example, as the "responsible" older sibling, we may have been put in charge of our younger brother or sister when we really wanted to be outside playing with our friends. Or you may recall a time that your mother or father found something broken in the house and asked that ominous question, "Who's responsible for this mess?!" We knew that to claim responsibility meant that we had done something "wrong" and there was usually some punitive result or humiliation.

As a result we think that freedom means to be free of responsibility. By the time we get to adulthood, most of us have accumulated a sufficient amount of baggage associated with the concept of responsibility. Responsibility feels "heavy" rather than "free."

We think that freedom is associated with doing whatever we want whenever we want. Feeling carefree (free of caring) means living an "unburdened" existence. For example, we think that if we just had enough money, we would be free to do whatever we want. As long as we believe that our freedom and happiness are dependent on the absence of problems, the absence of commitments, our economic circumstances or the actions of others, we will never be free or happy.

And as long as we think that responsibility is something to be avoided we are creating a personal breeding ground for our own victimhood, helplessness and powerlessness.

Shifting the Context

"People are always blaming their circumstances for what they are. I don't believe in circumstances. The people who get on in this world are the people who get up and look for the circumstances they want, and if they can't find them, make them."
- George Bernard Shaw

The way in which we think about something allows us to shift our experience, to essentially place ourselves in an empowered position. Albert Einstein once said, "You cannot solve a problem at the same level of thinking in which the problem was created." What this means is that if we don't change our thinking, the future will be just more of the past. This is not freedom. Freedom has more to do with our ability to change the way we think and the way we relate to the circumstances of our lives. From this understanding, our freedom is always here and now, in our own hands. To create a shift in our experience, we need to shift the context in which we understand and frame our experience. To capture a powerful context in which to hold the reality of responsibility we must understand one thing first: **responsibility is a choice**. It cannot be imposed or demanded. It occurs as an inevitable outgrowth of a choice for freedom and a willingness to account for what we choose and what we claim as our own. When we do this, we will experience and confront ourselves, our fears about making decisions, our self-doubt, our need for approval and our willingness to own our own power.

Responsibility starts with a willingness to accept that we are the source of our own experience: we are at "cause" in the matter of who we are, what we do, and what we have.

It is a way of being in the world in which we choose to relate to everything that shows up in our lives from a stance of responsibility; to see ourselves as "cause" rather than "effect."

This means:

- Facing and relating to any situation in a constructive way. Rather than re-acting (acting the same way over and over again) to the situation, we look to see what the appropriate action is in the moment. What is the action that would be most productive and beneficial now? We respond to the present rather than react from the past.

- Seeing every situation from the standpoint of "excellent learning opportunity! What can I learn from this?" Every situation in our life, whether pleasant or unpleasant, holds the opportunity to teach us something. From our mistakes and even from other people's mistakes we are able to inform the choices that we make in our future. Thomas Edison invented over one thousand versions of the light bulb before he invented the one that worked. Disappointments are great learning opportunities!

- Claiming the results, whatever they are, and seeing your part in any situation. We all have a tendency to focus "out there" on what the other people did or didn't do. However, if something is showing up in your life you can look and say "Hmmm, I wonder what this has to do with me?" To point your finger at others is like being in a boat that is leaking and saying, "I'm not going to do anything, the leak is on your side of the boat!" This includes both positive and negative results. Sometimes it is even more difficult for us to own the positive results in our life.

- Owning that you are the source of your own experience. This means not blaming others. This does not mean "blaming yourself." True responsibility has nothing to do with blame. You don't take responsibility because something is your "fault." You take responsibility because you choose to relate to everything in your life from a perspective of responsibility. This is the commitment you hold yourself to. This also opens the door for others to look at their part rather than to react defensively. However, whether they choose to claim responsibility or see themselves as a victim is their business.

- Making the connection between yourself and any outcome. When you take responsibility, you begin to see the connections between the way things are showing up and the result of your own choices, actions, thinking, attitude and behavior. As a result, you can change what isn't working. If you can't see the connection between yourself and the outcomes of your life, you will not know what to do differently. You will just continue to do the same thing and get the same result. As author Rita Mae Brown once said, "Insanity is doing the same thing over and over again expecting a different result."

- Seeing yourself as the source of:

how people perceive you and how you perceive others
your failures and your wins in life
your interpretations of life

Responsibility Creates Possibility

When you stand in the "world of responsibility," new possibilities emerge! It is just one possible attitude among an infinite array of choices. Other choices include: "I am a victim, it's not my fault, I can't do anything about it, I'm wrong, you're wrong, the world is wrong." The feelings that go along with these choices include anger, resentment, fear, powerlessness, hopelessness, helplessness, cynicism and depression. A stance of responsibility empowers you in ways that these other attitudes do not:

It puts the steering wheel of life back into your own hands.
It gives you more control over your own happiness and your life.
It allows you to shape and create your future the way you want it.
It allows virtually any experience or circumstance to be one of learning and opportunity.
It takes your attention off your complaints and moves you to positive action and the results you want.

The feelings and experiences that go along with this choice include clarity, empowerment, lightness, flow, energy, aliveness and joy.

Often we take responsibility only when we can find **proof** of our part. "I'll believe it when I see it," is our stance. In the matter of personal responsibility, there is no "proof" for it, there may be no evidence for it. You take responsibility purely out of choice, because that is how you choose to relate to the situation. It is not "true," or "right," or "better" to declare yourself responsible. Taking responsibility simply opens possibilities that other attitudes do not. When you believe it, you'll begin to see it.

True Responsibility Brings You Freedom!

So now we can see why the only way off of the drama triangle is through the gate of personal responsibility. In order to shift the dynamic you have to be able to see the part that you are playing and to choose to relate to the situation from a different perspective. The first thing to check is in what way are you seeing yourself as a victim? Where are you blaming the other person? What do you think their point of view is? Here are some questions that help:

* What in the other person's point of view about me is true? Can I see the way they see it?

- What in my point of view of them is not true? How is what I am thinking about them not really the whole story?

- What am I making up, assuming or imagining about them, especially about their intentions, or what they are really up to. Can I absolutely know beyond any doubt what their intention is?

We tend to want to see our slice of a story—our point of view, what they did to us. What we don't want to see is "the whole story," what came before that, what else is at play. We don't want to see our part. We want to avoid or minimize our part in the problem and amplify their part. Remember that from their perspective they are doing the same thing. Even if we see them as having the "bigger half" we still need to see that without our part, there is no bigger half. Ultimately, we need to look at the drama that is playing out on the stage of our life and ask ourselves the question: What is this play doing on my stage?

What is it about me that would make this situation likely? What is it about me that would require this drama? Questions like this make us aware of our unconscious thoughts. Our conscious thoughts are like the tip of an iceberg: about 10 percent of the whole. The rest of our thoughts, beliefs and ideas are the underlying assumptions that guide our lives. We don't question our unconscious thoughts because we are not aware of them, we only experience them as "the truth", as reality itself. So whenever there is a situation that you can't imagine that you "ordered up" from the universe, you have an opportunity to look and find the unconscious thinking that is driving your participation and experience.

A hallmark of the difference between someone who is sane and someone who is insane is the ability to question our own thoughts. The ability to look and say, "Is the way I'm seeing it really the truth?" "Is there any other way to look at this?" "Is there something

I believe about this situation or person that may not be the whole truth?"

As we do this, an amazing thing begins to occur. We begin to have a different experience of the situation, person or of ourselves. We step out of "being sure" or "being right" about them. And new possibilities begin to emerge. Out of this we can begin to choose a more productive interpretation and course of action.

We discover an astonishing truth: That the actual source of all of our experience comes from inside of ourselves—our interpretations, beliefs and ideas. As we open up to new perspectives, our experience of life changes.

12

Sex!

The attempt to reconcile eroticism and domestic life has been the source of many books, articles, seminars and couples therapy for the last few decades. Keeping desire alive in the familiarity of long-term relationships is something that most couples find challenging; many marriages have ended over this issue. The story of sex in modern couples is often a narrative of dwindling desire and a long list of excuses. Yet the ability to sustain sexual energy in the relationship is a source of vitality to both individuals and to the health of the marriage. Relationships that lose their 'juice" tend to fall into more platonic ways of relating and often leads to the arising of erotic feelings outside of the marriage. In one report, 2010 statistics on infidelity are as follows:

Percentage of men who admit committing infidelity in any relationship they've had: 57%
Percentage of women who admit committing infidelity in any relationship they've had: 54%

Another report estimates that roughly 30 to 60 percent of all married individuals (in the United States) will engage in infidelity at some point during their marriage (Buss and Shackelford).

For this reason the discussion of sex in marriage and the fate of eroticism over time is an important part of this book. Most couples are afraid to broach the subject of sex in conversation and as a result, they are not getting the sex they want in their relationships. In most of the couples I've worked with, people want more sex, less sex, better sex, hotter sex, more sensual sex, more connected sex, more fun with sex, more loving sex, more conscious sex, more passionate sex, and so on, yet very few people are talking about it or doing anything about it other than complaining. We wonder if we really turn our partner on, if they are really satisfied with our sexual exploits, if they came, how long it takes for them to come, how often they come, what they really want, what their fantasies are, what they are doing in their head and what they are feeling while we are making love.

Since we cannot have our partner's sexual experience of us, it is only through dialogue that we can discover these things! So how do we talk about sex? Talking about sex can be difficult even for partners who have been together for a long time. One of the primary considerations of any intimate conversation is that we feel safe enough to have the conversation. Judgments, analyses, condemnations, criticism and any kind of shaming is guaranteed to shut down any conversation for a long time, if not permanently. Having uninterrupted, private space is crucial. Creating an ambience that feels safe and intimate is also important. Talking about sex during sex is different than talking about it at other times. Some people are more comfortable with one than the other. Yet most people find sex awkward to discuss and even more awkward to do anything about. Partners who have been together for a long time and have established sexual patterns in terms of frequency, style, positions, location, often find it hard to bring up the idea of change. We are afraid of how our partner might react. We are afraid of what they might think. We are afraid of embarrassing ourselves or them or of having our ideas rejected. The thought of doing something "off the beaten path" often brings up anxiety and shame. This is particularly true if your favorite flavor of sex is not "vanilla." Having edgier, more dynamic sexual activity invites us to explore elements of ourselves that we may not normally adventure into. Sex is one of the places in our relationships and in our lives where we can let go of the images and masks we wear in normal everyday society and play more on the fringes of our own personalities. The willingness to engage with our own aggression, our letting go, our playfulness, our outrageousness, our power and our willingness to surrender control all make for more interesting sexual experiences. Think about the best sex you ever had. What was it about the person you were with? What was it about you? How was it different?

One of my clients we'll call Mary, had not had sex with her husband for ten years. She had had a hysterectomy and they had not had sex since. At first it seemed that the pain or discomfort associated with having sex after the surgery was the problem, but as we discovered, they had never explored the simple solutions of lubricants or alternatives to intercourse. She and her husband had a "nice, pleasant, friendly," platonic relationship. They both "agreed" that sex was not essential to the marriage. How convenient! Now nobody had to push the edge. End of conversation. They both avoided having to be uncomfortable again by bringing the subject up. They could just continue on "ignoring" their own sexuality and the impact of avoiding sexual feelings on themselves and each other. The impact is often a loss of "juice," aliveness and vitality to the relationship and to each of the individuals. Women who disconnect from their own sexuality tend to become more masculine in attitude and demeanor. They may get very work-driven. The men become more feminine and docile.

As we dug deeper into the issue, we discovered that having been raised Catholic, Mary had learned that sex was "bad" and that she was bad for liking it during her early childhood sexual explorations and play. In order to be "good" again in the eyes of her parents, she had to act disinterested in sex, and later, as a wife, she had to be a "good girl" during sexual activity. How much fun do you imagine she had in bed as a good girl? "Good girl sex. That sounds like some pretty boring sex to me," I said. She laughed. She realized that it was easy for her to just leave sex out of her life and continue on the way it was. "Is that what you really want?" I asked.

"No" she said. But because she and her husband had established a long standing pattern of a sexless marriage, it took some time for her to broach the subject with him. This generated quite a bit of anxiety for her, but when they finally talked about it, he was game! They lit some candles, bought some lubricant and began to explore their sexuality with each other again. This brought an energy back into their marriage that had been gone for years.

Sexless marriages are more common than you'd think. Many couples report having sex less than a dozen times a year. Recent reports indicate that this could be as many as 30% of couples! Couples who have frequent sex throughout their marriage report being sexually active well into their later years. I know one couple in their eighties who still have sex almost every day! They happen to be my parents, so I have this on record! Sexy octogenarians are a real possibility!

Couples with healthy thriving sex lives are able to shed inhibitions with each other, negotiate boundaries and encourage each other's sexual exploration.

The biggest thing that gets in the way of this is our attempts, both conscious and unconscious, to "normalize" things, to create a sense of familiarity and safety in the relationship. Minds like predictability. Minds tend to fear the unknown and therefore try to keep things in the realm of "the known." The willingness to step outside of our normal behavior and to explore new possibilities and new elements of ourselves, brings up anxiety for most people. We may feel frightened whenever our partner does anything differently, even if it is a change in the way they dress or eat. We want to know, "Why are you doing that?" We need a reason. We need to be able to analyze their behavior and figure out why they do what they do in an attempt to give ourselves some sense of control and security. We are afraid if we act "differently" than we have in the past we will be judged as being weird, bad or wrong. Some people are afraid to show intense excitement, sexual or otherwise, and the intensity of their feelings to someone they really love and respect. We don't want to be considered dirty, rude, crude or slutty by our partner. We want to have sex while maintaining our pure image of ourselves with our partner! Again, "good girl" or "good boy" sex can be pretty boring.

Our sex life is a safe playground in which our "images" and personas can fall away as we explore the deeper, more loving and more provocative aspects of ourselves. Boredom in the bedroom, as in life, generally speaks to a lack of imagination or the desire to play it safe by hiding our full eroticism from our partners.

Although men and women have similarities in terms of sexual desires, there are also ways in which we are very different. For example, for men sex is often a "one act play." They can often go from having a stressful day or working on a project to being "ready" for sex immediately. For women, getting in the mood and being emotionally and physically ready for sex takes longer. It's more like a "five act play." In fact, according to Louann Brizendine, M.D., psychologist, neurologist and author of The Female Brain, given a women's brain chemistry, it takes her about twenty-four hours to be ready for sex. She has to think about, get in the mood, and be able to relax. Additionally, if she is stressed out, anxious, or if she's had an argument and is mad at her partner, it's almost impossible for her to have much in the way of sexual feelings. So guys, if you are planning to have sex with your partner, be sure to not get into any arguments for twenty-four hours or you'll have to start the clock all over again! Speaking your partner's "love language" prior to sexual activity creates a mindset that is more likely to engage your partner's sexual desire. (See section on Love Languages).

According to Dr. Brizendine, "The sex related centers in the male brain are about two times larger than parallel structures in the female brain...That probably explains why 85 percent of twenty to thirty year old males think about sex many times each day and women think about it once a day or up to three or four times on their most fertile days. This makes for interesting interactions between the sexes. Guys often have to talk women into having sex. It's usually not the first thing on women's minds."

As noted sex therapist and author Esther Perel puts it: "Female eroticism is diffuse, not localized in the genitals but distributed throughout the body, mind and senses. It is tactile and auditory, linked to smell, skin, and contact; arousal is often more subjective than physical, and desire arises on a lattice of emotion."

Again, lead time, preparation and speaking the love language of your partner can help generate the mood that gives rise to sexual feelings. This next section includes a series of questions and assignments for communication about sex. It is designed to open up honest conversation between you and your partner. You can each write down your answers to these questions and then read them to each other. Or you can just discuss each question. If speaking about some of these things is too uncomfortable you can write them down on a piece of paper and hand it to your partner to read. Start wherever you are.

The following questions will begin to open up places where dialogue can occur.

Do you talk openly about sex with your partner? If not, why?

How important is sex to you in the relationship? What does it do for you?

What would make your sex life more satisfying to you? Or are you completely satisfied with your sex life?

These are three things I would like to try if my partner is open to the idea:

1.

2.

3.

One of my favorite fantasies is....(describe in detail).

Do you feel that you can ask your partner for what you want sexually? If not, why?

Do you feel comfortable with your own body sexually? If not, what might make you more comfortable?

How would you feel about your partner telling you what they want sexually?

How often do you like to have sex? What time of day?

Discuss the following with your partner:

Something I've always wanted to try is:
Some of the things I really love to do to my partner are:
Some of the things I really love him/her to do to me are:
Three things that get me in the mood for sex are:
Three things that most turn me off from sex are:
Three things that really help me achieve orgasm are:
It usually takes me between ____ and ____ amount of time to come to orgasm.

Sex toys or props I enjoy using include:

____

____

____

Discuss with your partner the ways in which you like to use sex toys and props. If there is anything that your partner does not feel safe with, you will need to come to agreement about how you can make it safe for them so they'll want to participate or find an acceptable alternative. For example, if you like to tie your partner with silk scarves, they may feel safer if the knots come easily undone or if one hand is free. While role playing or playing out fantasies it is important to have a "safe word" — a word that means STOP when either person uses it. That way if you want to say "no" as part of the fantasy, your partner doesn't confuse it with the word "STOP" or whatever safe word you use to indicate that you really want them to stop whatever they are doing.

I love sexy communication in the form of:

> *Examples: Speaking, emails or texting, cards, gifts, phone calls.*
> *I really enjoy seeing my partner wear:*
> *Examples: Sexy lingerie, tight jeans and top, all dressed up*

I am mostly aroused by:

> *Visuals (pictures, seeing my partner's body, etc.)*
> *Audio (hearing my partner say sexy things to me)*
> *Tactile (being touched or teased physically – be specific: lightly, firmly, where?)*
> *Smell (my partner's body odor, certain perfumes or scents, etc.)*
> *Other*

Here are more great conversations to have with your partner. This will reveal more about what you each enjoy:

> *What was the "naughtiest thing" you ever did sexually?*
> *What was the most fun thing you ever experienced sexually?*
> *What was the most romantic thing you ever experienced sexually?*
> *What was the most outrageous thing you ever did sexually?*

What are a few of your most repeated sexual fantasies? Discuss whether any of these are fantasies that you would actually like to play out with your partner. Many times we have fantasies that we really would rather not experience in real life—we just enjoy the fantasy. However there may be elements of the fantasy that you would like to play with. And there may be fantasies you would like to explore playing out with your partner. Discuss this with your partner. For example many women who have fantasies involving rape obviously don't actually want to be raped. In their fantasies the "rape" is usually with someone they can imagine being sexual with and they are never beaten up or hurt. Most women enjoy being "ravished" by their partner and having their partner take control. However, this may be a different story for women who have actually experienced sexual abuse in their past. Letting go of control and taking control are elements of the power play in sex that make for erotic sexual dynamics and partners can take turns with the roles of power, control and surrender in sex. People who have positions in life in which they may have much responsibility and control often enjoy various forms of fantasy and sex play that involve surrender and letting go, as the bedroom can become one place where it is safe to do so.

Fun Assignments:

Show your partner how you like them to touch you.

Show your partner how you touch yourself so they can learn what turns you on.

Give each other a full body massage.

Schedule date nights where you make romance and sex a priority. Prepare for this ahead of time (remember the 24 hour rule!)

Share with your partner the things you have written about in this section and find out how they would answer these questions.

This week, create the best sexual experience you've ever had with your partner. Plan it out together or one of you plan it and surprise the other! Think about what leads up to it in the days preceding the event. Remember, sex is not a one-act play for women!

Take turns during sexual exploits where one of you in totally in charge and the other practices letting go andsurrender.

Have the Sex Life You Want

The idea that sex must be spontaneous, that it is only the result of chemistry, the heat of the moment, or something that "just happens" keeps us from having to take responsibility for creating the sex life we want. Planning and giving thought to sex takes time and some effort. Committed sex is intentional sex. It requires that you deliberately include it in your life and that you bring yourself to it rather than waiting for it to "show up." The early stages of romantic love may appear to be spontaneous but in fact, sex is often the "climax" of many days of thinking and planning—we decide what to wear, where to go and imagine what we will do with our partners. It may seem spontaneous when it happens, but we've actually been planning it all out in our heads. So to continue to have a vibrant sex life in marriage you must be willing to consciously include sex as an important element of your relationship and your life. Not from an attitude of duty and obligation—nothing is less erotic than obligatory sex! But because it is something you want and you choose to take responsibility for creating what you want in your life. Fantasize about your partner and then co-create your fantasy!

As Esther Perel says in her book, Mating in Captivity, "Complaining of sexual boredom is easy and conventional. Nurturing eroticism in the home is an act of open defiance." It is the willingness to challenge yourself to step out of your comfort zone and out of ambivalence toward pleasure that will create the sexy marriage you want.

On the road of marriage and family, don't forget to enjoy yourself! If you are not enjoying yourself, then notice what you are doing instead. Complaining about not enjoying yourself? Commit to take the action necessary to create the relationship experience you want.

Question your assumptions about sex!

13

Give Up All Hope...

One of the important distinctions to make in a relationship is the difference between hope and desire. There are things we want from our partner and generally speaking, there are things we will get and things we won't get. When you select a partner you are selecting them as they are, not for who they will become when you are done molding them into who you want them to be. The more you are waiting for them to change, get a clue, see the light and finally become the person you "know' they can really be "with your help," the more frustration and disappointment you will experience and the more dissatisfaction you will have in your relationship. Ultimately you must look at the person you are with and ask yourself this question: "With no change at all, would I take them as they are?" If the answer is yes, then the relationship can work. If the answer is "no" or "yes, but..." it probably won't work out.

Notice if you take who they are "personally." For example, your partner may be a workaholic. Do you think "if they loved you enough" they wouldn't be? Or is your partner someone with a negative attitude toward life who might be happy if you were "good enough?" Is this person commitment-phobic and you think "if they really got who you are" they would commit? This kind of thinking is completely misplaced. It is the same kind of thinking that children have when their parents divorce and they think, "Gee, if only I'd been a better kid they would have stayed together." It is a kind of narcissistic thinking that fails to recognize that people are who they are with or without you. When you squeeze an orange you get orange juice. You get orange juice no matter who squeezes it. It's like saying, "If this orange really loved me, it would make apple juice!" You cannot change someone's basic personality. If you think it's so easy to do that, just try to change yours. If you can do that successfully, go tell your partner how you did it. And send me a letter about it too. The point is that while we can make requests of people, we must understand that the general nature or tendencies of each person are something we cannot change. We must accept them or end the relationship.

The only possible exception is if you are with someone who is <u>actively</u> working to change something about themselves. For example, a tennis player who wants to improve his game may take tennis lessons and practice. Another example is someone who cuts certain foods out of their diet in an effort to improve their eating habits. Basic elements of people's personalities are much, much more difficult and complex to change. They are the results of a lifetime of development and they don't change because we—or they— want them to. It takes work, often some kind of therapy or personal coaching and usually quite a bit of time. If someone has a pattern of infidelity in their life, don't think it will be different "because they are with you now." That is magical thinking. Personality and behavioral patterns are not about you. They are about them. I met my husband at a personal growth workshop on relationships. He was a divorcee and disclosed to me at some point that he had had multiple affairs during his marriage. When we got together I was sure that this wouldn't be a problem with us because we were doing so much personal growth stuff and because our relationship would be very different than his first marriage. Oh well! Eight years later the pattern emerged again. The part that was most fascinating to me is that I was surprised!

If there is something about your partner that you think "needs fixing" and that you're the one who can do it, you are in for a big surprise. In the first place, there is a problem with looking at your partner as if they are a "home improvement project." A fixer-upper—something that with repair and remodeling could be really a nice place to live! If you do not find your partner to be a "nice place to live" as they are, you should probably move. This is my advice: Give up all hope. See who you are with. Face the truth of it. All of the stuff you like and the stuff that bugs you. Then accept this fact: "This is who they are." Once you have accepted this, ask yourself the question: If nothing about them ever changes, is this someone that I would like to spend my life with? Can I be with them without trying to change them? If the answer is yes, try this experiment:

For the next thirty days, don't do anything to try to change, fix or correct your partner. Watch who they are and practice lovingly accepting what shows up. Then see how you feel. Are you more stressed? Less stressed? Notice what happens for you when you stop trying to change them.

Question your assumptions about how "they should change."

14
Committing to Practices

One successful aspect of my counseling work has been helping couples make the shift from "committing to the other person" to "committing to being the kind of person who can have the relationship that I want." This means a commitment to practicing the skills and behaviors of conscious relationship, rather than trying to focus your commitment onto your partner or something outside of your control.

In the Art of Living, Epictetus, the Roman philosopher (circa 55 – 135 CE), taught that, "Happiness and freedom begin with a clear understanding of one principle: Some things are within our control and some things are not." It is only after we have faced and accepted this fact that we can experience more peace of mind and personal effectiveness in our lives and in our relationships with others. In the category of "what is in our control" are our own behaviors, aspirations, choices and actions. "Outside of our control" are the behaviors, aspirations, choices and actions of everyone else, including our loved ones. We experience confusion and frustration in our lives when we try to control things that are naturally out of our control. We mistakenly think we are successful in life to the extent that we can control other people and events.

However, our success in life is largely determined by our ability to see what is actually in our control and to focus our attention and use our power there.

To the extent that we try to control our partner or other people and events, we experience ourselves as ineffective and powerless. Our own commitments are among the things that are under our control. What are you committed to? Make sure that your commitments are in the area of your control. For example, I can commit to being supportive of my partner. However I cannot commit to "making him happy" as another person's happiness is not in my control. I can commit to practicing the skills of generous listening, but I cannot control whether or not you are honest with me. I can commit to being honest with you, but I cannot control whether or not you listen to me. I can't commit to never being attracted to another person because we don't control our biological feelings, but I can commit to only expressing my sexuality in my relationship with my partner.

Feelings of attraction are not in our control but what we do with our feelings are.

Exercise:

- What things in your relationship are naturally in your control? What is not?

- What do you want to commit to? You will find that these are generally in the realm of behaviors and skills.

For example:

I commit to being personally honest.
I commit to reliably keeping my agreements.
I commit to the honest expression of my feelings.
I commit to expressing my sexuality only with my partner.

I commit to actively practicing good listening skills in my relationship.
I commit to resolving conflict in ways that are respectful.
I commit to clear up anything that gets in the way of our feeling close.

As you do this you will find that the things you commit to are doable, and that they can improve over time. It is a good idea to take on the commitment to practicing good relationship behaviors and skills in the spirit of learning rather than in the spirit of perfectionism. We understand that we and our partner are doing our best and that we can support ourselves and each other in the growth of our relationship skills and in our growth as individuals. We begin to develop ourselves into people who are skillful in relationships.

It's interesting to think of the idea of "relationship skills." Yet they are skills. Some people are very good in relationships and some people bring poor habits and skills to their relationships. Why is that? One reason is that pretty much everything we know about relationships we learned in our families of origin. So if we were lucky and our families modeled healthy ways of relating and communicating, we will have learned how to do that too. If they modeled problematic behaviors, then that is what we learned.

Since relationship skills are not taught in school, we had nowhere else to go to formally learn them, and unless we made deliberate efforts through some kind of formal or informal training, we would never have learned those skills. Which is why we become adults who may still be lacking good relationship abilities. But the good news is that it is learnable. We learned what we do now. And we can learn new things that may work better for us and for our partner and for the kind of relationship we want to create. Elements of relationship skills that are important for good relationships:

Communication
Conflict resolution
Sex and eroticism

Emotional Intelligence
Parenting
Listening
Making and keeping healthy agreements

Obviously, if you've gotten this far in your relationship, you have developed some skills in these areas. As you become even better, you will naturally improve the quality of your marriage just by virtue of the fact that you are bringing stronger capacities to the relationship.

15
Identifying Our Core Values

Core values are what make life worth living. They reflect the way in which we want to live in the world, how we want to relate to others, and how we want others to relate to us. If our goals in life answer the question WHAT? Our core values answer the question, HOW? In what way do we wish to go about accomplishing our goals so that the fulfillment of our goals is meaningful? Not the achievement of the goal itself, but the experience of living our values in the process of getting there. The way in which we do things creates the experience we have of everything we do. When we participate in work or play with others and we do this with integrity, we experience a certain pride in ourselves and the way we show up. Being in integrity allows us to be more grounded and focused, rather than rationalizing our disingenuousness or over-thinking our reasons and excuses for not showing up as we said we would. Recent studies in the field of psycho-immunology report that the inability to act consistently with our own personal values takes a significant toll on our immune system! In other words, our lack of integrity, our lack of acting in ways that are consistent with our real values literally makes us sick. Organizations that unite around a noble cause or mission and a set of core values, are healthier, happier, more productive work places with better bottom line results.

Couples who bond around their core values and life purpose also experience greater success in creating meaningful, happier relationships. The discussion of core values in a relationship is important as it guides us and our partner in how we each wish to be treated and considered by each other and what really matter most to each of us. In this next section, I will ask you to give thought to your own personal core values. Although we each have many values, there are usually about five that are "core." Author Jim Collins describes the answer to this question his "acid test" on core values: "If it were to cost you time or money to hold this value, would you continue to hold it?" If not, perhaps that value is not really "core." In other words, time and money are more important than this value. I would also add "approval" to that list. If acting from your core values risked some approval from your partner or friends, would you do it anyway?

This does not mean that it is always "easy" to hold our core values. We are challenged by competing values and pressures from the outside. As we get in touch with what our values are, it allows us to take a stand and to act in accordance with them. In this way we show up as most true to ourselves. Our values become our guidelines for how we act and how we make decisions and choices.

Here is an exercise to do with your partner: Tell a story about something positive that happened in your life. Something that was really wonderful. Together, capture the values that are present in your story. What made it wonderful, and from that, what things can you deduce are important or meaningful to you?

Now tell a story about something negative that happened in your life. Something that was really a bummer. Again, capture the values that are present. What elements made it a bummer? And from that, what are the things that are important or meaningful to you?

Repeat this process by telling six stories each: three positive and three negative.

Then identify the following:

What are the three to five values in life and in relationships that are most important to you?

Example:

Honesty
Making a contribution to others
Being respectful to others
Honoring differences
Doing what I say I will do
Doing things with integrity
Kindness, Generosity, Compassion

Which of the values you came up with do you want to see present in your relationship/marriage?

Pick the top three to five that are most important to you.

Now define them according to what you mean by them and how it looks in action.

Example: Honesty: "Reliably telling the truth without being prompted. Even when it is uncomfortable, we tell each other how we really feel, what we really want and what we really believe. We do this knowing that this can cause the other to feel mad or sad or scared but we do it anyway, because we choose to be real with each other. We continue to communicate honestly and in the process to clear up and resolve our differences."

Define each of the core values you've selected.

Under what circumstances would you find it difficult to uphold your values?

Give examples of the kind of situations where it is hardest for you to really demonstrate your own values:

> *It's hard for me to be honest if I think it will make someone mad or sad.*
> *It's hard for me to be kind when I am angry.*
> *It's hard for me to be respectful if I feel that I strongly disagree with someone.*
> *It's hard for me to stay in integrity if there is something I want, and I can make a lot of money by doing something that is not completely honest.*
> *It's hard for me to keep my agreements and do what I say consistently, especially because I tend to do things at the last minute which can cause me to be late.*

These things represent your own personal growth edge in living your values.

Think of the times in your life where you have "fudged" on your own values even when you have given yourself "a darn good reason." What excuses do you use? Write these down so that you can know the "road signs" when you are about to go out of integrity on your own values. If you share this with your partner, you can support each other in living your values rather than rationalizing your way out of them. Rationalizing is what we do instead of telling ourselves the truth.

Example: In my last relationship I didn't tell my husband the truth about things because I decided it would just upset him and I wanted to keep the peace. The truth is, I was afraid to deal with the possibility of him being mad at me and I wanted to avoid my own discomfort.

How can you support each other by being aware of each other's values? How can you encourage each other by being aware of each other's values?

As you make decisions together in life, look and see, are these choices in alignment with our core values?

Question your decisions and choices to make sure they align with your core values!

16
In Closing

Some of the key learnings for me in the matter of my marriage and divorce were:

1. You cannot control anyone else's choices, desires or behavior. The attempt to do so is crazy-making for both people.

2. We love who we love and there is nothing we can do about it.

3. Nobody has power over me or my happiness.

4. The way that relationships "happen" for me are a direct reflection of my internal reality. To change what happens on the outside, I need to change what is occurring on the inside.

In my life I have noticed that every time I think that the source of my happiness is in something outside of myself, that thing goes away. This has been true with people, money and situations. Although I wish that my "life lessons" had happened in gentler ways, I've noticed that it has left me with the awareness of who is left when the dust clears. That would be me. Our source of happiness lies where we would least expect to find it: inside of ourselves.

When we get that, we can share our happiness with others and give them the freedom to come and go in our lives as is appropriate for them and us. The coming and going of people in our lives is the way of it. Think of all the people in your lifetime that have come and gone. Letting go is a practice. We "hold on" and then we let go. When we finally stop trying to control our relationship we find out if we actually have one.

What finally freed me in my marriage was this recognition. I truly didn't "need" my husband. I thought I did, but I went on retreat and sat with the question "Is that really true?" for about ten days and let the answer come from within. When I realized that I didn't need him in order to be happy, or in order to be anything, it brought me to my true source of happiness which is love itself. I realized that I didn't have to stop loving anything or anyone and that love just is – always here, already present. And the more I could just love life as it shows up, exactly the way it unfolds, with the comings and goings of all the people and events in my life, the more I just loved the whole thing. The joy, the love, the anger, the grief—I wouldn't trade a moment of it. It's called A Full Life. In hindsight, every seeming "disaster" of my life has resolved gracefully and gotten me to where I am and who I am today. The support of life itself is already here and always is, even when it doesn't feel like it.

When I really got that, I went back to my house with no agenda at all. I walked in the door and saw my husband sitting in the living room and realized that I hadn't seen "him" in months. Just my story of him and his betrayal and how he'd "ruined everything." And then I saw this sweet guy just sitting there reading a book. "Oh there you are!" I said, as though I was seeing him after a long spell. "So what are we doing? Married? Divorced? What do you think?" It no longer mattered. After a trial separation we agreed to get a divorce. We contracted an attorney and worked out our own settlement. On the day we signed the papers we sat in the attorney's waiting room holding hands and chatting. When the attorney came out and saw us he said, "Are you sure you want to do this?" He'd never seen a couple getting a divorce holding hands and talking.

After we signed the papers we went to lunch and then we each headed out to the next chapter of our lives.

Try the practices in this book and discover for yourself what is possible when you question your thinking and assumptions and play the game of conscious relationship, rather then just acting out the past. Relationships comprise the most significant part of our emotional lives. Be willing to do the work that is needed to have the quality of relationship you want. There are no guarantees about the future, but you can really improve your odds. I'll bet on it.

Resources

The Hendricks Institute www.hendricks.com

The Five Love Languages www.5lovelanguages.com

Brent Kessel www.brentkessel.com

Bruce Lipton www.brucelipton.com

Productive Learning Workshops www.productivelearning.com

www.ingramcontent.com/pod-product-compliance
Lightning Source LLC
LaVergne TN
LVHW021519080426
835509LV00018B/2562